Battles of Armageddon:

Debates on Bible Prophecy

Battles of Armageddon:

Debates on Bible Prophecy

by Mark Johansen

Electric Tactics

Monroe, Michigan

Battles of Armageddon: Debates on Bible Prophecy
Copyright © 2018 by Mark Johansen
All rights reserved

ISBN: 978-0-983085935
Library of Congress Control Number: 2018904976

Cover credits:
"Wailing Wall" by Mark Johansen
"Grable" (mushroom cloud) courtesy Federal Government of the
United States, National Nuclear Security Administration Nevada Site
Office Photo Library, number XX-12.
"America From Space" courtesy National Aeronautics and Space
Administration

Questions or comments about this book may be sent to:
mark@electrictactics.com

Contents

Prediction is very difficult. Especially about the future.

-- Neils Bohr

Detailed Contents

1. Plan

1.1. The Problem

This is a book about the Second Coming of Jesus Christ.

Christians have been looking forward to Jesus's Second Coming for almost 2000 years. We know that he is coming back because the Bible tells us so.

And right there, we run into a problem.

Much, probably most, of what the Bible teaches is very clear and straightforward. When we are told, for example, "Thou shalt not commit adultery", there is little room for confusion. Only people trying to evade the clear command ask, "But what if I don't love my wife anymore?" When the Bible says that Jesus selected twelve disciples, we don't need to ponder whether this might mean eleven or thirteen or a hundred.

Of course many people don't believe that the Bible is true and authoritative. When the Bible tells us that Joshua made the Sun stand still and that Jesus changed water into wine, many doubt that these things really happened. When the Bible condemns worship of other gods, or homosexuality, many people say that this is intolerant and they don't see anything wrong with such actions. But the plain words of the Bible clearly say that these miracles happened and these rules should be followed. The writers of the Bible are claiming that these things are true. If you don't believe them or don't agree with them, that's fine, we can certainly debate whether the Bible is true or false and present evidence for either side. But no serious, honest person can say that the Bible is unclear on these points.

Some people pretend that the Bible is vague and confusing about these things. When they don't like a command in the Bible and don't want to follow it, instead of honestly saying, "I don't recognize the Bible as authoritative and I disagree with this", they will claim to respect the Bible but then say that it is just so hard to figure out what it really means. When the Bible says, "thou shalt not commit adultery", does that mean never ever? Or not unless we really love each other, or if my wife isn't satisfying me anymore, or if I feel like it? They come up with contorted arguments why the words don't mean what they say, but this is very complicated and full of many layers and shades of meaning, and that understanding what God really said requires deep and careful study. And of course they always have some deep insight that proves that the Bible really says the opposite of what those simple-minded people think it means.

The fair answer to such people is, "No. When the Bible spells something out in plain, simple language, it means what it says."

But when it comes to discussions about the Second Coming, the Bible *is* confusing and difficult to understand.

It would be nice and convenient if Bible prophecies clearly said, "On June 14, 2035, a man named Fred Stover will be born in Pittsburgh, Pennsylvania, who will become governor of the state and who will sign a law called State Bill 132B, which will ..." etc. Some Bible prophecies are very clear and specific like that. But most aren't. I think anyone who has read and tried to understand Bible prophecies will agree that most are frustratingly unclear and subject to multiple interpretations.

Every now and then someone challenges me on this point.

They'll say, "Oh no, the prophecy is completely clear and obvious. You just have to understand it in light of this passage over here, and take into account these historical events, and apply my 42 principles of Biblical interpretation", etc. To which I say, Your interpretation may be correct, but it is not clear and obvious. The fact that it takes you three hours to explain why it is obvious proves that it is not obvious.

1.2. My Solution

So: Many Bible prophecies are hard to understand. This means that people have come up with many competing theories of interpretation.

In this book, I take many of the questions that have come up about the Second Coming, and present all the competing theories that I know of. I try to present all theories fairly regardless of my own opinion.

I present few firm conclusions. My goal with this book is to summarize many different ideas, and help the reader to draw his own conclusions.

There is one thing that makes me particularly well-qualified to write such a book: I don't claim to know the right answers!

I've been reading about Bible prophecy and studying Bible prophecy for over 40 years, since I was a teenager. I've heard lots of theories come and go. When I was younger I thought I knew all the answers. But the more I've studied, the more I realize I don't know. When I am preparing to teach a class or write a book, of course I study the subject, and sometimes, often, things that were unclear to me before become clear. I come to conclusions where previously I was confused. I thought that working on this book might lead me to some conclusions about the Second Coming. In fact it's mostly done the opposite. As I studied the arguments for theories that I had previously dismissed, I began to see their merits. There are several issues where I thought I knew the right answer, but after further study, now I am not so sure. There is only one question where I started out unsure and now I think I know the right answer – I'll mention it when we get there.

Often when a writer presents competing theories, even if he doesn't tell you outright, it's obvious which theory he thinks is correct. He presents the best arguments for the theory that he likes and skims over its weak points, while hammering on the flaws in theories he dislikes. Of course some writers are good at presenting opposing views fairly. Personally, I think the worst case is when a writer tells you that he is presenting opposing views fairly, while in reality he is stacking the deck in favor of his preferred theory.

So maybe by being (I hope) well-informed but still undecided, I can give a more balanced presentation. I think that on most of these questions, there are many theories that all have merit, so I can present them all fairly. I don't have to try to hide or counteract my biases, because I don't have many biases.

On some questions I have come to conclusions in my own mind. And of course there are some theories that I think are stronger than others. In this book, I will plainly tell you when I have drawn conclusions. This does have the risk of unduly influencing the reader to agree with me. But I think it's the more fair way to present the information. If I frankly tell you which side I'm on, you'll be forewarned to judge my presentation accordingly.

By the way, I have a lot to say about some theories, and very little about others. The amount of space I give to a theory has little to do with how convincing I find it. Some theories are just simple and easy to explain, while others … aren't.

1.3.   Ground rule number one

For purposes of this book, I am assuming that the Bible is inspired by God and that it is true.

I am well aware that there are many people who do not believe that the Bible is true. In other contexts, I am happy to debate the evidence for and against. (I've written one book on that subject and I hope to write others if I live long enough and my brain holds out.)

But I'm not going to go back to the starting point with every conversation. I'm starting here assuming that the reader is a Christian and believes the Bible, or is interested in knowing what Christians think. If you think that the Bible is a bunch of superstitious nonsense, this book isn't for you. Except maybe to add to your list of Christian beliefs to make fun of.

So in this book, I'm not going to consider any challenge to the authority of the Bible. When discussing whether some theory about the Second Coming is true, the most basic test I will use is, "How well does this theory stack up against what the Bible says?" I will seriously consider, "Maybe we are misinterpreting the Bible", but not "Maybe the Bible is a bunch of fairy tales."

This book is unapologetically written from a Christian perspective. It is primarily from an evangelical Protestant perspective, though I discuss Catholic views with respect.

At times I make blunt statements about various religious groups – some might say harsh. Bear in mind that I am presenting the views of various different schools of thought. Sometimes I agree with them; sometimes I don't.

But when, for example, I say that Jews were wrong to reject Jesus as the Messiah, obviously I realize that Jews don't agree with that. This is not intended as an insult to Jews, but as a frank statement of a very fundamental disagreement.

In a few places I say that the Catholic Church in the Middle Ages became corrupt. Some Catholics agree that this was a dark time in their church's history, others defend it. That's a debate for another time. The point here is that some theories of prophecy are based on the idea that the Catholic Church became corrupt, and it is impossible to discuss them without saying that.

1.4. Variations

In this book I'll discuss a number of different theories about many different questions.

There's a common joke that comes up about almost any

controversial subject: If you ask 10 people you'll get 11 different opinions. That's true of theories about Bible prophecy.

So let me make the disclaimer now that when I state what proponents of a theory claim, when I say "Preterists believe that ..." or "Pre-Tribulationists say ...", I am describing what I understand to be the most common or distinctive view among advocates of a given theory. There are almost always going to be disagreements about details even within the group. So just because I say "Pre-Tribbers believe that ...", and your pastor calls himself a Pre-Tribber, it does not necessarily follow that this particular person believes exactly as I have described it. Likewise, please don't send me nasty letters saying, "Hey, I'm a Pre-Tribber, and that isn't quite what I believe."

So for the sake of brevity, I am not going to constantly say "most advocates of theory X believe this, but of course there are variations and some say other things". I'll just say, "Theory X says this."

Of course if I've grossly misstated the essential idea of some group, feel free to correct me. I think I've accurately stated what various groups believe; I've tried to be accurate; but if I've messed up, I'd like to know about it.

1.5. Credit

For the most part, I won't discuss which famous writers or preachers advocate this or that theory, or who first proposed a theory. I'll just discuss the theory.

I do this because most of the theories I will discuss are broad ideas that have been taught by many theologians, and that are believed by many people today and/or in the past. In many cases it is hard to say who first thought of a particular theory. And even if you could, these theories have changed and developed over time. It might be interesting to trace the origin and development of these theories. But that would be a totally different book. Frankly, when writing this book I didn't want to get bogged down in months of research to definitively prove who first suggested an idea, just so I could write the one sentence, "this was first proposed by so-and-so".

Furthermore, if I said, "this theory as proposed by so-and-so", then I trap myself into discussing that particular person's version of the theory, even if others have explained it better or some variation has become more popular. I base my descriptions of each theory on what I have read and heard from a variety of sources.

I do this cautiously because I am concerned about failing to give credit where it's due. I certainly don't want to plagiarize other people's work or to appear to do so. Perhaps I should make one point clear right now: I do not claim to have originated any of the major theories presented in this book. The only contribution to the subject I claim is to present all these competing theories side by side, and hopefully to shed some light on their relative merits. In a few places here and there I mention variations on theories that might be mildly original ... or maybe I've just rediscovered what others have said a million times.

So I mention specific writers, preachers, and theologians when it's relevant to a point I'm trying to make. But otherwise, I treat each theory as common knowledge.

1.6. Important side note: Salvation

Need I say it? I don't think that your position on any question about the Second Coming is fundamental to salvation. I gladly fellowship with people who have widely differing views on these questions.

I sometimes wonder just how wrong someone can be in his understanding of Scripture and still be saved. I don't know exactly what God's criteria are here.

Romans 10:9. That if you confess with your mouth the Lord Jesus and believe in your heart that God has raised Him from the dead, you will be saved.

So clearly, at the one extreme, I have a hard time imagining how someone could not believe that there is a God and that Jesus is God come to Earth and still be saved. At the other extreme, I don't see how you could read Romans and say that God would deny someone salvation because he has a wrong opinion about who wrote the book of Hebrews.

I think wrong ideas about interpretation of complex Bible prophecies fall more in the second category. If someone has a theory about, say, if and when the Rapture will happen that proves to be wrong, I don't think God will punish him for that. I certainly can't imagine that that will cost him his salvation. I suppose that many sincere Christians will be quite surprised when Christ returns. Some will have been sure up to that moment that his coming was still decades or centuries away. Others will have been expecting him to arrive in some totally different way. But I don't think that God will hold this against them. The Bible doesn't say, believe in Jesus *and* have the right beliefs about all these other doctrines, and you will be saved.

I'm sure that there are things that I believe that will turn out to be wrong. Of course I don't know what. If I knew that something that I believed was wrong, than that would mean that I really didn't believe it, right? But if you asked me to list all the things I believe to be true, I'm sure I could list thousands of things, from the nature of God to the law of gravity to my brother's address. I don't doubt that among all those things that I think I know, some number are wrong.

2. The Big Questions

Let's start by looking at the disagreements on the highest level, the most fundamental questions. We're not going to get into the arguments pro and con here. We'll save that for when we get into the details. But I just want to set the stage for the most basic disagreements in interpretation.

2.1. Figurative or Literal

Some things in the Bible are clearly intended to be understood literally. To take a deliberately trivial example, when we read Matthew 13:1, "On the same day Jesus went out of the house and sat by the sea", we understand this to mean that Jesus was in a literal house, that he walked out of the house, and that he sat down by a literal sea. We do not speculate what the house and the sea might represent, or discuss the possible spiritual significance of houses and seas. This is a simple statement of an event that happened just as described.

Some things in the Bible are clearly intended to be understood figuratively. To again take a deliberately trivial example, when we read Psalm 18:2, "The Lord is my rock and my fortress and my deliverer; My God, my strength, in whom I will trust; My shield and the horn of my salvation, my stronghold", we understand this to be a figurative description of the power and protection of God. We don't suppose that God is literally a rock or a horn. These are just analogies to describe how God is solid and reliable and protects his people.

This is not something that only applies to the Bible. We all routinely use a mix of literal and figurative speech. Most of the time we don't even think about it. Suppose one of your friends didn't show up for some planned get-together, and he offered as an excuse, "I had to work late yesterday. The boss is a real slave-driver," You would immediately understand that the statement about working late was intended literally, and the statement about the boss being a slave driver was intended figuratively. Your friend really, literally did have to work late. (Or at least, he wants you to believe that he did.) But you surely don't suppose that his boss is literally holding people as slaves. This is a rhetorical exaggeration.

Usually it's obvious what is figurative and what is literal. Occasionally a person will make a literal statement and someone else will think they meant it figuratively, or vice versa. There are lots of jokes based on this idea. Like a young man tells his friends, "My new girlfriend is a real doll", and the next scene we see him kissing an inflatable dummy. In real life it's rare, but it happens.

But when it comes to Bible prophecy, we often run into this problem that we can't say for sure what is literal and what is figurative.

We'll look at a number of examples of this throughout this book. But just to make clear what I'm talking about:

Sometimes it's plainly spelled out that a prophecy is symbolic. For example, in Daniel 7, Daniel sees a vision of four strange creatures. Then an angel explains the vision to him: He is told that the creatures represent kingdoms, that the horns on their heads represent rulers of those kingdoms, and so on. We are plainly told that the monsters are not to be taken literally. This isn't a prophecy that Godzilla is going to destroy Tokyo. Rather, they are symbols. They represent empires.

I don't know of a prophecy where the text says, "this isn't a symbol, this is literal". But sometimes the words are so plain that a literal interpretation seems almost certain to be intended. For example, in Matthew 24, Jesus says, "For many will come in my name, saying, 'I am the Messiah', and they will deceive many. You are going to hear of wars and rumors of wars. ... For nation will rise against nation and kingdom against kingdom. There will be famines and earthquakes in various places." Etc. These statements all appear quite literal. There will be actual false Messiahs, actual wars, actual earthquakes, and actual famines. There is no reason to believe that these are symbols, that "wars" really means doctrinal rivalry and "earthquakes" really means social change or anything like that.

But other prophecies are puzzling. Revelation 11:1-14 describes "two witnesses" who will preach during the end times. Some Christians interpret these to be two literal male human beings. Others think that they represent Jews and Christians, or two churches.

2.2. Preterist or Futurist

"Futurism" is the theory that there are many prophecies in the Bible about events that are still in our future, i.e. that as of the 21st century these prophecies still have not been fulfilled. The opposite is "Preterism", the theory that most or all of the prophecies in the Bible have already happened, that these prophecies have already been fulfilled.

Most Futurists see the Second Coming as the end of the world, or at least, the end of history as we know it.

Some Preterists don't believe in a Second Coming in this sense. They believe that prophecies that have been interpreted to describe a Second Coming really refer to major events in history, but not the end of history. People in this group are called "Full Preterists".

Other Preterists believe in a Second Coming in the same

sense that Futurists do, but they believe that many prophecies that Futurists say are about the Second Coming are really about past events. These are called "Partial Preterists".

Most conservative Christians are Futurists.

Sometimes the difference between Preterists and Futurists is described as, "Futurists believe that Bible prophecy is still in the future; Preterists believe all prophecy has already been fulfilled." But this is a little over-simplified.

I don't think anyone believes that all the prophecies in the Bible are about events that are still in the future. There are many prophecies that have clearly already been fulfilled. The prophecies about Israel being conquered by the Assyrians and the Babylonians (for example Jeremiah 29:1-10) were fulfilled thousands of years ago. The prophecy about the Messiah being born in Bethlehem (Micah 5:2) was fulfilled when Jesus came. Et cetera. So in a sense, no one is a 100% Futurist.

Some prophecies are almost certainly still in the future. Revelation 21:1 talks about the Earth being destroyed. As the world is still here, it seems obvious that this prophecy has not yet been fulfilled. You could say that this prophecy is not talking about a literal destruction of the Earth but is symbolic in some way. But few Preterists go that far. (Though some do. See section 6.13.) So there are few 100% Preterists.

So a more serious description of the difference is this:

The key Bible prophecies under debate are the prophecies of Daniel, Matthew 24, and Revelation.

Futurists believe that large sections of Daniel and most or all of Revelation is future. Most say that Matthew 24 was partly fulfilled when the Romans destroyed Jerusalem in AD 70, but that the bulk of it is future. Some say all of it is future.

Full Preterists say that Daniel, Matthew 24, and Revelation have all been fulfilled. They say Daniel was fulfilled by Alexander and his successors, from 336 to 160 BC, and that Matthew 24 and Revelation were fulfilled when the Romans destroyed Jerusalem in AD 70.

Partial Preterists say that most of Daniel and all of

Matthew are already fulfilled, while parts of Daniel and Revelation are still future.

Or to put it another way: Futurists believe that these prophecies refer to one specific event or period, the Second Coming, when Christ will return physically and establish his kingdom on Earth. As understood by Futurists, when this Second Coming happens, no one will be able to say, "Is there really a God?" or "Is Jesus really the Son of God?" It will be obvious that he is ruling the world.

Full Preterists believe that God will continue to work basically the same as he has worked in the past: nations will rise and fall, some people will worship him and some will reject him, that the evidence will be there for those who want to see but that people will still be able to make a credible case for doubt, and so on.

Partial Preterists believe that there will be a Second Coming, but that many prophecies that Futurists say are about the Second Coming are really about other, past events.

2.3. My premises

As I said, I don't claim to know the right answers to most of the controversial questions in Bible prophecy.

But I have come to a few conclusions on the big issues. So, be warned, here are the premises I bring to the table.

I think that when in doubt, we should generally assume that a prophecy is literal.

Of course some prophecies are symbolic. In some cases the symbols are spelled out for us. For example, in Daniel 2:1-45 we are told of Nebuchadnezzar's dream of a statue. (I won't quote it here. If you're not familiar with the story, please look it up.) God gives Daniel the interpretation: the status represents a series of empires that will come to power. The statue is a series of symbols.

But it's easy to say that a prophecy must be symbolic as a way to explain away scriptures that don't fit our theories. If it's literal, that pretty much ties it to one meaning. But if it's symbolic, than we can debate what the symbols mean, and with sufficient creativity we can make the prophecy mean almost anything. I think many honest, well-meaning Christians fall into the trap of saying that something in the Bible is symbolic because they don't like the literal meaning or it doesn't fit their theories. When I hear two competing theories, and theory A interprets the Bible literally while theory B interprets it symbolically, I lean toward A.

Second, there's a danger of saying "I don't see how this could be literally true, so it must be figurative", when in fact we just don't have enough imagination, or enough faith. Perhaps the best example of this is prophecies about Israel. For almost 2000 years, Christians said that *of course* prophecies about the future that talked about Israel couldn't be referring to a literal nation of Israel, because that nation had been destroyed. So these prophecies must be using Israel as a symbol for something else. Perhaps they are really talking about the Church, or about some other nation. Then in 1948 the nation of Israel was re-established. Suddenly it became clear that a literal interpretation of these prophecies *is* possible.

It's exciting to see an ancient prophecy like that fulfilled in our own time. But there's a danger here. It's tempting to try to interpret current events to fit a Bible prophecy, or interpret a Bible prophecy to fit current events. As I'm sure you're aware, well-meaning, honest Christians have been predicting that Christ would return within the next few years -- for hundreds of years. When these predictions turn out to be wrong, it gives non-Christians a justification to laugh at us. It weakens the power of the Christian message.

Thus, while I am certainly interested when I see a parallel between current events and a Bible prophecy, I think we need to be very cautious about concluding that we are seeing the fulfilment before our eyes. Exciting if true, but too many Christians have jumped the gun too many times.

Before we conclude that a prophecy is being fulfilled today, or that we are seeing the groundwork for it to be fulfilled in the near future, we should examine if this particular prophecy might not already have been fulfilled in the past. This can be hard work, as it requires a detailed study of history. And let's be honest with ourselves: It's a lot more fun to say, "Wow, the king described in this prophecy may be the current U.S. president in office right now!" than to say, "Wow, the king described in this prophecy may be Antiochus Epiphanes, who ruled the Seleucid Empire in 175 BC!"

My daughter once called me at work and asked, "Dad, are you a Preterist?" I replied, "I'm a tentative, partial Preterist." We then discussed prophecy until I had to get back to work.

A Preterist is someone who believes that most or all of the prophecies in the Bible have already been fulfilled. (See section 2.2.) I think a number of prophecies that many modern Christians believe will be fulfilled in the near future were actually fulfilled thousands of years ago. Thus, I tend to be a Partial Preterist. I'll discuss specific examples as we get there.

(I think my kids and I have more interesting conversations than most families.)

2.4. Partial fulfillment

A trap that some Christians fall into is the idea of "partial fulfillment". They want to apply some prophecy to the future because it fits into the grand theory that they are building. But the prophecy fits something that happened in the past too closely to dismiss as coincidence. If they admit the prophecy has already been fulfilled, then they can't use it as part of their scheme of future fulfillment.

So they say that the past fulfillment was "partial fulfillment". Yes, this prophecy was already fulfilled, but it will be fulfilled again in the future in a different way. For example, I read one book on prophecy that said that, yes, the prophecies in Daniel about future empires were fulfilled by the Persian Empire and Alexander the Great, but they will be fulfilled again in the future in a totally different way by Russia and the Antichrist.

I think this is stretching. For the most part, if a prophecy was fulfilled in the past, then it's done. The mystery is solved. We shouldn't expect God to recycle his prophecies.

Two caveats:

One, there is a difference between "partial fulfillment" in the sense that the same prophecy will be fulfilled multiple times in different ways, and "partial fulfillment" in the sense that part of the prophecy has been fulfilled and part has not. For example, Daniel 2 has a prophecy about a series of empires that will come in the future – Daniel's future, that is, they are all in our past now. They are normally interpreted to be the Babylonian, Persian, Greek/Macedonian (Alexander the Great), and Roman empires. So at the time of, say, the Persian empire, half the prophecy was fulfilled and half was still in the future. There's nothing strained about suggesting that parts of a prophecy have been fulfilled and parts have not.

Two, there is at least one occasion in the Bible where a prophecy apparently *does* have such a double fulfillment.

> Isaiah 7:14-16. Therefore the Lord Himself will give you a sign: Behold, the virgin shall conceive and bear a Son, and shall call His name Immanuel. Curds and honey He shall eat, that He may know to refuse the evil and choose the good. For before the Child shall know to refuse the evil and choose the good, the land that you dread will be forsaken by both her kings.

You have probably heard this quoted as a prophecy about Jesus. Matthew quotes this verse as a prophecy about Jesus being born to a virgin (Matthew 1:22-23).

But in context, Judah was being attacked by an alliance of two nations: Ephraim (the northern Jewish kingdom) and Syria. The prophet Isaiah assures King Ahaz of Judah that God will not allow these two nations to defeat Judah. As a sign, he says that a child will be born in the very near future, probably to some young woman who was standing there at the time, or who Isaiah and the king knew, and that before that child grew to be old enough to "know to refuse the evil and choose the good", these two kings would be defeated and Judah would be saved. And indeed, both kings were assassinated soon after and the attack on

Judah abandoned.

Jews traditionally put the age of being expected to know good from evil at 13 for boys and 12 for girls. Modern Jews often have a ceremony called a "bar mitzvah" (boys) or "bat mitzvah" (girls) to celebrate the child reaching this age. So the idea of the prophecy is: King Ahaz, the people you fear so much will both be dead within 13 years. (Ahaz didn't heed the prophecy and instead sought help from another nation, Assyria. This alliance cost Ahaz and his nation big time as the Assyrians made constant demands for money and political concessions in exchange for their military help.)

Some commentators say that the woman in question was Isaiah's wife, others that she was Ahaz's wife, and yet others that she was simply a woman who happened to be there at the time. Like, "Hey Ahaz, you see that young lady standing across the street over there? Well, she's going to have a baby in a few months, and ..." Almost all commentators, Jewish and Christian, say that the fulfillment in Isaiah's time was not a virgin birth. The word translated "virgin" has multiple definitions: it can mean a woman who has never had sexual relations, or it can mean any young woman. Even if we understand it to mean "virgin", Isaiah may have meant that she is a virgin now, but she will get pregnant in the usual way very soon.

So the prophecy was fulfilled twice: Once in the child born as a sign to Ahaz, circa 750 BC, and then again in the birth of Christ.

I should add that some Christian commentators reject this double fulfillment explanation as strained for exactly the same reasons that I find other such double fulfillment explanations strained. They then try to come up with some explanation to fit a prophecy about the Messiah into the context. Jews routinely reject the idea of a double fulfillment and say that this prophecy was fulfilled centuries before Christ and that Christians are twisting the prophecy to try and make it about the Messiah.

2.5. Common symbols

As we walk through Bible prophecies, we'll see some common symbols come up repeatedly. For example, both Daniel 7 and Revelation 13 use animals or monsters to represent nations and horns on those animals' heads to represent rulers of those nations. Both Isaiah 51 and Matthew 20 use the idea of a cup from which someone must drink to represent punishment for sin.

If we see "thing X" used in one prophecy and we are told that it is a symbol for Y, and then in another prophecy we again see thing X with no explanation, it is fair to at least theorize that it is again a symbol for Y.

2.6. Quality of Symbolism

I taught a series of Bible studies on the parables of Jesus once, and as I studied for that lesson, I was really struck by the quality of Jesus's parables.

Consider the Parable of the Evil Tenants.

Matthew 21:33-41. "Hear another parable: There was a certain landowner who planted a vineyard and set a hedge around it, dug a winepress in it and built a tower. And he leased it to vinedressers and went into a far country. Now when vintage-time drew near, he sent his servants to the vinedressers, that they might receive its fruit. And the vinedressers took his servants, beat one, killed one, and stoned another. Again he sent other servants, more than the first, and they did likewise to them. Then last of all he sent his son to them, saying, 'They will respect my son.' But when the vinedressers saw the son, they said among themselves, 'This is the heir. Come, let us kill him and seize his inheritance.' So they took him and cast *him* out of the vineyard and killed *him*. Therefore, when the owner of the vineyard comes, what will he do to those vinedressers?" They said to Him, "He will destroy those wicked men miserably, and lease *his* vineyard to other vinedressers who will render to him the fruits in their seasons."

Notice some interesting things about this parable.

Every symbol that Jesus used in the parable had a meaning. The landowner is God. We are told in verse 43 that the tenants are Israel, especially the priests. The servants are the prophets. The son is Jesus. Etc. Nothing is out of place. We don't find ourselves asking, "But wait, who does this 'son' represent?" or "What does it mean when he says he'll lease the land to someone else?"

Every detail of the parable relates to the "inner story" that Jesus wants to convey. Yet at the same time, the "surface story" makes sense. We have no trouble imagining why tenants don't want to pay the rent. We don't ask in bewilderment, "But why would the landowner send people to collect the rent?" or "Why did he get so angry when they killed his son?" The reasons are obvious. The story is plausible.

Compare Jesus's parables to other parables and allegories.

Perhaps the most famous parable from ancient times, outside of the Bible, is Plato's Parable of the Cave. It's pretty long, but here are some key excerpts:

> "Next, then," I said, "take the following parable of education and ignorance as a picture of the condition of our nature. Imagine mankind as dwelling in an underground cave with a long entrance open to the light across the whole width of the cave; in this they have been from childhood, with necks and legs fettered, so they have to stay where they are. They cannot move their heads round because of the fetters, and they can only look forward, but light comes to them from fire burning behind them higher up at a distance. Between the fire and the prisoners is a road above their level, and along it imagine a low wall has been built, as puppet showmen have screens in front of their people over which they work their puppets."
>
> "I see," he said.
>
> "See, then, bearers carrying along this wall all sorts of articles which they hold projecting above the wall, statues of men and other living things, made of stone or wood and all kinds of stuff, some of the bearers speaking and some silent, as you might expect."

"What a remarkable image," he said, "and what remarkable prisoners!"

"Just like ourselves," I said. "For, first of all, tell me this: What do you think such people would have seen of themselves and each other except their shadows, which the fire cast on the opposite wall of the cave?"

"I don't see how they could see anything else," said he, "if they were compelled to keep their heads unmoving all their lives!"

"Very well, what of the things being carried along? Would not this be the same?"

"Of course it would."

"Suppose the prisoners were able to talk together. Don't you think that when they named the shadows which they saw passing they would believe they were naming things?"

"Necessarily."

"Then if their prison had an echo from the opposite wall, whenever one of the passing bearers uttered a sound, would they not suppose that the passing shadow must be making the sound? Don't you think so?"

"Indeed I do," he said.

"If so," said I, "such persons would certainly believe that there were no realities except those shadows of handmade things."

"So it must be," said he.

"Now consider," said I, "what their release would be like, and their cure from these fetters and their folly; let us imagine whether it might naturally be something like this. One might be released, and compelled suddenly to stand up and turn his neck round, and to walk and look towards the firelight; all this would hurt him, and he would be too much dazzled to see distinctly those things whose shadows he had seen before. What do you think he would say, if someone told him that what he saw before was foolery, but now he saw more rightly, being a bit nearer reality and turned towards what was a little more real? What if he were shown each of the passing things, and compelled by questions to answer what each one was? Don't you think he would be puzzled, and believe what he saw before was more true than what was shown to him?"

. . .

"Very good. Let him be reminded of this first habitation, and what was wisdom in that place, and of his fellow-prisoners there; don't you think he would bless himself for the change, and pity them?"

"Yes, indeed."

"And if there were honours and praises among them and prizes for the one who saw the passing things most sharply and remembered best which of them used to come before and which after and which together, and from these was best able to prophesy accordingly what was going to come—do you believe he would set his desire on that, and envy those who were honoured men or potentates among them? Would he not feel as Homer says, and heartily desire rather to be serf of some landless man on earth and to endure anything in the world, rather than to opine as they did and to live in that way?"

. . .

"Then we must apply this image, my dear Glaucon," said I, "to all we have been saying. The world of our sight is like the habitation in prison, the firelight there to the sunlight here, the ascent and the view of the upper world is the rising of the soul into the world of mind; put it so and you will not be far from my own surmise, since that is what you want to hear; but God knows if it is really true. At least, what appears to me is, that in the world of the known, last of all, is the idea of the good, and with what toil to be seen! And seen, this must be inferred to be the cause of all right and beautiful things for all, which gives birth to light and the king of light in the world of sight, and, in the world of mind, herself the queen produces truth and reason; and she must be seen by one who is to act with reason publicly or privately."

— Plato, *The Republic*

So okay, we get the idea: Plato believed that what we perceive as reality is just a shadow of true reality.

But compare this parable, as an allegory, to Jesus's parables.

Some of the symbols in Plato's parable are clear: the prisoners in the cave are the human race. The shadows on the wall are our perception of reality. The objects that the puppeteers carry on the road are the true reality.

But many of the elements in the parable do not clearly symbolize anything. What is the fire that casts the shadows? What is the road that the puppeteers walk on, or the wall between them and the prisoners? What are the bonds that keep the prisoners facing in one direction?

The surface story makes no sense at all. Why would someone lock these men in a cave and leave them to watch shadows on the wall? Why would puppeteers march around with objects to cast the shadows? How do the prisoners eat? If guards feed them, can't they see the real food and the guard who gives it to them — or at least his hands — and not just shadows? How do they go about giving each other prizes if they are all locked in place and can't move? Etc. The surface story doesn't stand on its own.

Have you ever tried to make up an analogy? Perhaps to explain some point about a technical subject, or to make a political argument. Did your analogy hang together as well as Jesus's do? My guess is probably not. I often use analogies to make a point, and every now and then someone will point out how the symbols in my analogy don't hang together, and I end up saying, Yes, yes, the analogy isn't perfect, but my point is …

When God uses symbols in a prophecy, I think that, just like Jesus's parables, we should expect every symbol mentioned to stand for something and to make sense in context. Any attempt to interpret the prophecy that says, "Well, yes, he mentioned a crown, but I don't think that means anything …" is probably inaccurate.

That said, let me clarify that I don't think we should extend a parable or symbols beyond what is presented. I mean, for example, in the parable of the tenants that I began this section with, presumably on a real vineyard it rains now and then. What does the rain represent? Probably nothing. Jesus did not mention rain when he told the parable. It is not one of the symbols that make up the parable. We can't add things that aren't in the original story and expect them to necessarily fit.

2.7. Synthesis

Students of prophecy often theorize that several prophecies are about the same person or event.

For example, Daniel 9:26 talks about "the prince who is to come". 1 John 4:3 talks about "the spirit of the Antichrist, which you have heard was coming". And Revelation 13:1 talks about "a beast rising up out of the sea, having seven heads and ten horns" who we are told (Revelation 17) represent an empire or the ruler of that empire. Many Christians believe these are all talking about the same person.

Or: Daniel 9:27 talks about the "70th week", a period of seven years of divine judgment. Matthew 24:21 talks about a "great tribulation". Revelation 7:14 also talks about a "great tribulation". Many Christians believe these are all talking about the same period of time.

Of course it is fair to compare prophecies, look for common elements, and theorize that two prophecies are talking about the same thing. There's no reason to suppose that God is only allowed to talk about each thing once! But we should be careful that we do not take these theories as absolutes. Just because many Christians suppose that two prophecies are about the same thing doesn't make it so. Perhaps these "many Christians" are wrong.

For example, I think most evangelical Protestants would

say that Revelation is all about the Antichrist and a seven year period of tribulation. If someone knows nothing else about prophecy, they know that. Right? But in fact, Revelation never uses the word "antichrist". That word is only used in 1 and 2 John. And while Revelation talks about a period of "tribulation", nowhere does it say that this tribulation lasts seven years. The only specific association of a time period with "tribulation" in Revelation is ten days (Revelation 2:10).

It is certainly possible that the Antichrist described in 1 and 2 John and the Beast described in Revelation are the same person. It is certainly possible that the 70th week of Daniel and the Great Tribulation of Matthew and Revelation are the same event. But nowhere does scripture say this. These are theories, interpretations.

We'll discuss a number of cases of such "syntheses" in the following chapters, with arguments for and against each.

3. A Brief History of the World

3.1. Introduction

There are some events in history that come up repeatedly in discussions of Bible prophecy. A few key prophecies mention specific time periods, so for an interpretation to be plausible the times have to match up.

So to help in discussing prophecies that are or may be related to past historical events, here is a list of events that routinely come up. You may find it helpful to refer back to this list when events are mentioned.

Please note that there is often debate among historians and archaeologists about exact dates. Some of the dates I give here are highly reliable, but others are debatable. It is unlikely that any of these dates are off by more than 10 or 20 years.

3.2.   A Note on Notation

"BC" stands for the "Before Christ". "AD" stands for "Anno Domini", which is Latin for "the year of our Lord".

Some people think that "AD" stands for "After Death". This is simply mistaken. It's not English: it's Latin.

Today it's common to write the year followed by either BC or AD. Logically, and in the original usage, BC was written after but AD before. That is, we say, for example "100 years Before Christ", but "The year of our Lord, 100". So in this book I follow the old convention of BC after but AD before.

3.3.   Date Arithmetic

BC dates are basically like negative numbers and AD dates are like positive numbers, except that there is no year zero. The year after 1 BC is AD 1. If we do conventional arithmetic, 1-(-1)=2. But doing year calculations, AD 1 – 1 BC = 1. So if you're taking the difference between an AD date and a BC date, do the arithmetic normally, and then subtract 1 from the number of years to account for the fact that there is no year 0. If you're adding a number of years to a BC date and it takes you into AD, do the arithmetic normally and then add 1, to account for the fact that you have to skip over the 0.

3.4.   Dating the Life of Christ

The AD/BC calendar was invented by a monk named Dionysius Exiguus in the year AD 525. He set AD 1 to be the year that he understood that Jesus was born (or possibly, conceived). Unfortunately, there is no surviving record of how he came up with this date.

Almost all modern historians believe that Dionysius got his dates slightly wrong. It's beyond the scope of this book to go into a long discussion of the dates of Jesus's life, but just to summarize:

Jesus's birth can be tied to events in the life of Herod. There are four men named Herod who were rulers in Judea: First was Herod the Great. After him his kingdom was divided among his three sons, Herod Archelaus, Herod Phillip, and Herod Antipas. Both Herod the Great and Herod Antipas are mentioned in the Bible, both simply called "Herod".

The Jewish historian Josephus wrote in his book *Antiquitities of the Jews* (book XVII, chapter 6), that Herod the Great died shortly after a lunar eclipse. The Bible discusses Herod hearing about the birth of Jesus and trying to have him killed. See Matthew 2.

Eclipses are very regular and predictable, so modern astronomers can tell us exactly when there were lunar eclipses that would be reasonable candidates for the eclipse Josephus speaks of. There are three plausible candidates: March of 4 BC, January of 1 BC, and December of 1 BC. Based on other dates in Jewish and Roman history books, most historians take the 4 BC eclipse as the most likely. Assuming this is true, Jesus would have had to be born in 4 BC or shortly before. Most historians put Jesus birth somewhere between 6 BC and 4 BC.

The Emperor Augustus wrote a summary of what he considered the great achievements of his reign, called "The Acts of Augustus". Number 8 on his list of achievements is that he commissioned three great censuses of the Roman Empire, in 28 BC, 8 BC, and AD 14. Luke says that shortly before Jesus was born:

Luke 2:1. A decree went out from Caesar Augustus that all the world should be registered

The 8 BC census might well be the one that Luke talks about. Bureaucracy was slow in those days as in these days, and communications were slower, so it could well have taken several years from when the emperor ordered a census to when it actually got underway in a remote province.

(By the way, critics of the Bible like to connect Luke's census to one that was conducted in AD 6 (and which Luke mentions in Acts 5:37), and then point out that this creates a problem because if Jesus wasn't born until AD 6, Herod would have been dead many years before Jesus was born, thus making the accounts of Herod hearing about his birth impossible. So yes, that can't be the census that Luke was talking about. It's not clear to me how the critics' mistake in identifying the census somehow proves that the Bible is wrong.)

According to Luke:

> Luke 3:1-2. Now in the fifteenth year of the reign of Tiberius Caesar, Pontius Pilate being governor of Judea, Herod being tetrarch of Galilee, his brother Philip tetrarch of Iturea and the region of Trachonitis, and Lysanias tetrarch of Abilene, while Annas and Caiaphas were high priests, the word of God came to John the son of Zacharias in the wilderness.

And then a little later he writes:

> Luke 3:23. Now Jesus Himself began His ministry at about thirty years of age ...

The implication is that Luke 3:23 happens not too long after Luke 3:1, probably within a few months. So Jesus's ministry began "in the fifteen year of the reign of Tiberius Caesar" or perhaps the sixteenth year.

Historians have a pretty good idea of when Tiberius began his reign: September 18, AD 14. So add 15 years to that and Jesus ministry began about AD 29. If he was born in 4 BC, then he would be 32, which matches Luke's statement that he was "about thirty".

The Gospel of John mentions three Passovers occurring during Jesus ministry – the last coming the day after he was crucified. As Passover comes once a year, Jesus's ministry lasted more than two years. (If the first Passover mentioned happened a few days or weeks after he began his ministry, and he died on the last one, it would be just over two years. If there was a Passover just before he started his ministry, it would be over three.) It's possible that there were other Passovers during which nothing important enough happened for John to mention, so it could have been longer. This, combined with other information, leads most historians to put Jesus death somewhere between AD 32 and AD 34.

Note that all these dates and times could be off by a year or two. For example, when Luke says that it was the 15th year of Tiberius's reign, is he counting the calendar year when Tiberius began to reign, so if he took office on September 18 then the following January 1 would be the "second year"? Or is he counting from anniversary to anniversary, so that the "second year" begins the following September? Tiberius's father-in-law, Augustus, made him co-ruler several years earlier, and so you could count his reign from the beginning of this co-regency rather than his sole regency. The 15th year could be anywhere from the first day of that year to the last day. Et cetera.

I think it's an interesting side note that unlike a fairy tale, Luke does not say this all happened "once upon a time". You often hear urban legends or conspiracy theories that are very vague about just when and where something happened, making it difficult to check the facts. But Luke gives very concrete historical references. So while we can't be sure of exact dates, we know within a few years. And while we don't know the exact address at which the events in Jesus life happened, we know the cities, and we can put those cities on a map. This is not something that happened "a long time ago in a galaxy far, far away". It happened in AD 29 in the city of Jericho, which is at latitude 31° North, longitude 35° East.

3.5. A List of Events

722 BC	Israel (northern kingdom) is conquered by Assyria.
597 BC	Judah (southern kingdom) is conquered by Babylon. Many Jews are exiled to Babylon, including the prophet Daniel.
539 BC	Cyrus of Persia conquers Babylon
535 BC	Cyrus issues a decree allowing the Jews to rebuild the temple.
530 BC	Book of Daniel written.

521 BC	The rebuilding of the temple is completed. Note the temple was rebuilt, but the city as a whole was still in ruins.
457 BC	Artaxerxes issues first decree to rebuild Jerusalem. However, opponents of the Jews then told Artaxerxes that the Jews were planning to revolt. He was tied up with a war and didn't want to take time to investigate or deal with the subject, so he halted the rebuilding.
445 BC	Artaxerxes issues second decree to rebuild Jerusalem. After the war, Artaxerxes was satisfied that charges against the Jews were false and he allowed rebuilding to resume.
334-323 BC	Alexander the Great of Macedonia conquers Greece, Asia Minor, the Middle East, Egypt, Persia, and parts of India, building what was probably the largest empire up to that time. After his death, his empire is divided among a number of his generals. The four strongest ultimately conquer or dominate the rest, leaving four empires: Cassander rules Macedonia and Greece; Lysimachus gets Thrace and western Turkey; Seleucus gets modern Iran, Iraq, Syria, and territories stretching out to India; and Ptolemy gets Egypt and Libya.
175-164 BC	Antiochus Epiphanes rules Seleucid Empire. In 167 he sacrifices a pig on the altar of the temple in Jerusalem.
20 BC	Herod's temple built.
4 BC – AD 34	Jesus lives
AD 37-41	Caligula rules Roman Empire. He tries to put a statue of himself in the temple in Jerusalem. The Jews resist, and Caligula dies before the order can be carried out.
AD 54-68	Nero reigns. First major persecution of Christians.
AD 66-73	Jewish War: Jews rebel against Rome. They lose. During the course of the war, in AD 70, Titus destroys the temple.

AD 81-96	Domitian reigns. Second major persecution. John is exiled to Patmos.
AD 85	Book of Matthew written.
AD 95	Book of Revelation written.
AD 132-136	Jews rebel again under Simon Bar Kokhba. Simon declares himself the messiah. They lose again. To prevent further rebellions, Hadrian razes Jerusalem to the ground, exiles all Jews from Israel, and builds a temple to Zeus on the site of the Jewish temple. Third major persecution, lasts 10 years.
AD 315	Roman Emperor Constantine has a vision of a cross in the sky and converts to Christianity. Ends persecution of Christians by Rome.
AD 687-691	Dome of the Rock, a Muslim shrine, is built on the site of the Jewish temple. It stands to this day.
AD 1517	Martin Luther posts his Ninety-Five Theses on the door of the church in Wittenberg. This incident is often taken as the start of the Protestant Reformation.
AD 1929	Vatican City becomes an independent country.
AD 1948	Israel is re-established as a nation.

4. Major Events and People

There are a number of events and people described in Bible prophecy.

We'll briefly list them here to give an overview. We'll be going into much more detail in the following chapters. The purpose here is just to introduce the main players so we have at least a general idea of who and what we're talking about.

The list shows the key Bible verses that mention each event or person. This is not intended to be a complete list: In most cases there are other verses that may (or may not) discuss the same thing.

4.1. Events

Abomination of Desolation	Daniel 11:31, Daniel 12:11, Matthew 24:15. A desecration of the temple. Exactly what it is is not clearly spelled out. Most scholars believe this refers to Antiochus Epiphanes sacrificing a pig on the altar of the temple in Jerusalem in 167 BC, or some sacrilege in a rebuilt Jewish temple in the future committed by the Antichrist, or both.
70 weeks	Daniel 9:24. A period of time that Daniel used as a framework to describe several major future events. As we'll discuss, almost all scholars agree that "weeks" here means "weeks of years", that is, intervals of seven years, so that Daniel is talking about a total of 490 years. This primarily relates the rebuilding of Jerusalem to the coming of the Messiah. Exactly when the last of the 70 weeks happens is debated.
Great Tribulation	Matthew 24, most of Revelation. An extreme divine judgment. Exactly when this happened or will happen, who is being judged, and the nature of the judgment make up one of the big debates that we will be discussing.
Millennium	Revelation 20. A period when Satan is imprisoned and Christ rules on Earth.
Rapture	Matthew 24:37-41, 1 Thessalonians 4:15-17. Christians are miraculously taken out of the world and up to Heaven to be with Christ.
Second Coming	Matthew 24, Acts 1:11, Revelation 19:11ff, many others. Christ returns to Earth in power and glory.
First & Second Resurrections	Revelation 20:4-6. Two distinct occasions on which the dead are raised.
Bema Seat Judgment	2 Corinthians 5:9-10, Romans 14:10-12. A time of judgement. The exact nature of the judgement is debated.

Great White Throne Judgment	Revelation 20:11-13. A possibly different judgement. This is clearly when the unbelievers are condemned to Hell.
New Heaven & Earth	2 Peter 3:10-12, Revelation 21:1. God destroys the Earth and creates a new Earth.
Armageddon	Revelation 16:12-16. A place where the enemies of God fight a final climactic battle against those who follow God.

4.2. People

Israel	Many references. God's chosen people. A nation made up of descendants of Abraham, Isaac, and Jacob.
Seven Churches	Revelation 1-2. A group of seven churches in the Roman province of Asia (modern Turkey) that the book of Revelation was originally addressed to. May also represent other churches throughout history.
Dragon	Revelation 12:3-9. A symbol for Satan. May also represent an evil empire.
Woman with the child	Revelation 12:1-2, 13-17. A person or group persecuted by Satan. Possibly Israel, possibly the Church, possibly someone else.
Prostitute of Babylon	Revelation 17. In older translations she is often called the "Whore of Babylon". A symbol for a city that is a source of evil and corruption. Often thought to also represent a corrupt religion or empire.
Antichrist	1 John 2:18-22, 4:3; 2 John 1:7. A leader of forces opposed to Christ. Many think he is a political leader.

The Beast	Revelation 13:1-9. An evil empire or leader that opposes Christ. Many believe that the Beast and the Antichrist are the same person. Note: There are actually several "beasts" mentioned in Revelation, Daniel, and other prophecies, but the beast of Revelation 13:1-9 is the one normally referred to as *the* beast when discussing prophecy.
False Prophet	Revelation 16:12-14, 19:19-20. An associate of the Beast who persuades people to worship the Beast.
Two Witnesses	Revelation 11:1-13. Two men – possibly two literal individuals, possibly symbols of two groups or organizations – who preach during the Tribulation, and who are ultimately killed by the Beast.
Man on the White Horse	Revelation 6:2, 19:11-16. The man on the white horse in Revelation 19 is clearly Christ coming in glory. The man on the white horse in Revelation 6 is sometimes also said to be Christ, but usually is equated with the Antichrist.

5. Timelines

5.1. Introduction

A key difference between different interpretations of prophecy is how each school of thought arranges the events on a timeline: which comes first, which comes second, and so on, and also which are past and which are future.

Indeed, the major theories are often identified by names that describe their proposed timeline. These names are based on the relationship between four key events: the Rapture, the Tribulation, the Second Coming, and the Millennium:

Pre-Tribulation: the Rapture occurs before the Tribulation.

Mid-Tribulation: the Rapture occurs in the middle of the Tribulation.

Post-Tribulation: the Rapture occurs after the Tribulation.

Combined with:

Premillennial: The Second Coming occurs before the

Millennium.

Postmillennial: The Second Coming occurs after the Millennium.

Amillennial: The Millennium is not a literal, specific period of time but a symbol.

And then there's the distinction we've already discussed:

Futurist: These events are all in the future, yet to be fulfilled.

Full Preterist: These events are all in the past, the prophecies already fulfilled.

Partial Preterist: Some of these events are past and some are future.

Once you lay out these events on a timeline, the position of other events tends to fall into place.

That said, here are the timelines of the major theories.

5.2. Pre-Tribulation / Premillennial

This is the timeline that most evangelical Protestants today prefer.

1. 69 Weeks
2. Jesus
3. Today
4. Rapture
5. Tribulation (7 years, = Daniel's 70th week)
6. Second Coming
7. Millennium (1000 years)
8. Armageddon
9. New Heaven & Earth

5.3. Postmillennial

This timeline was popular in the Middle Ages.

Under this theory, the Millennium began with the arrival of Jesus Christ and ends with the Second Coming. As more than

1000 years have now passed, modern Postmillenialists either say that the Millennium is not a literal 1000 years, or that it began (or will begin) sometime later than Jesus's first coming.

1. 70 weeks
2. Jesus
3. Tribulation
4. Millennium (1000 years), includes today
5. Armageddon
6. Second Coming
7. New Heaven & Earth

5.4. Full Preterist

1. 69 weeks
2. 70th week, includes Jesus ministry
3. New Heaven and Earth
4. Tribulation (AD 70)
5. Christ returns (not the Second Coming as most think of it)
6. Millennium (indeterminate length), includes today
7. No clues to future

5.5. Partial Preterist

1. 69 weeks
2. 70th week (includes Jesus)
3. Tribulation (AD 70)
4. Christ returns (not the Second Coming as most think of it)
5. Today
6. Second Coming
7. Millennium
8. New Heaven and Earth

Pre-Mil/ Pre-Trib	Post-Mil	Full Preterist	Partial Preterist
69 weeks	**70** weeks	**69** weeks	**69** weeks
✝ Christ	✝ Christ	✝ Christ	✝ Christ
 Today		New Heaven & Earth	
⇑ Rapture	Tribulation	Tribulation	Tribulation
Tribulation	 Millennium (Today)		Jesus returns *not* Second Coming
	Armaggeddon		Today
Second Coming	Second Coming	Jesus returns *not* Second Coming	Second Coming
 Millennium		 Millennium (Today)	 Millennium
Armaggeddon			
New Heaven & Earth	New Heaven & Earth		New Heaven & Earth

6. Details

6.1. Introduction

So, let's get to the meat.

In this section we'll go through the key events and people in Bible prophecy, and discuss various theories of what each means.

Note: I have tried to arrange these sections in an order that requires the minimum amount of references to things that have not yet been discussed. So the order may seem a little chaotic

6.2. Abomination of Desolation

Let's begin with the Abomination of Desolation.

The name is made up of two words that are rather obscure in English. "Abomination" means "something greatly disliked or abhorred", or "a vile or shameful action, condition, or habit". The word "desolation" means "devastation, ruin". (thefreedictionary.com) So an "abomination of desolation" is a shameful act that causes ruin.

Daniel 9:26-27. And after the sixty-two weeks Messiah shall be cut off, but not for Himself; And the people of the prince who is to come shall destroy the city and the sanctuary. The end of it shall be with a flood, and till the end of the war desolations are determined. Then he shall confirm a covenant with many for one week; but in the middle of the week he shall bring an end to sacrifice and offering. And on the wing of abominations shall be one who makes desolate, even until the consummation, which is determined, is poured out on the desolate.

Daniel 11:29-32. At the appointed time he shall return and go toward the south; but it shall not be like the former or the latter. For ships from Cyprus shall come against him; therefore he shall be grieved, and return in rage against the holy covenant, and do damage. So he shall return and show regard for those who forsake the holy covenant. And forces shall be mustered by him, and they shall defile the sanctuary fortress; then they shall take away the daily sacrifices, and place there the abomination of desolation. Those who do wickedly against the covenant he shall corrupt with flattery; but the people who know their God shall be strong, and carry out great exploits.

Daniel 12:9-12. And he said, "Go your way, Daniel, for the words are closed up and sealed till the time of the end. Many shall be purified, made white, and refined, but the wicked shall do wickedly; and none of the wicked shall understand, but the wise shall understand. And from the time that the daily sacrifice is taken away, and the abomination of desolation is set up, there shall be one thousand two hundred and ninety days. Blessed is he who waits, and comes to the one thousand three hundred and thirty-five days.

Matthew 24:15-21 Therefore when you see the 'abomination of desolation,' spoken of by Daniel the prophet, standing in the holy place" (whoever reads, let him understand), then let those who are in Judea flee to the mountains. Let him who is on the housetop not go down to take anything out of his house. And let him who is in the field not go back to get his clothes. But woe to those who are pregnant and to those who are nursing babies in those days! And pray that your flight may not be in winter or on the Sabbath. For then there will be great tribulation, such as has not been since the beginning of the world until this time, no, nor ever shall be.

Mark 13:14. (similar to Matthew 24)

None of these passages spells out exactly what the "abomination of desolation" is. Daniel links it to sacrifices, and in Matthew, Jesus links it to the "holy place", presumably the temple.

There are several historical incidents that might qualify as the abomination of desolation, and a suggestion for a future fulfilment.

Theory 1: Antiochus Epiphanes, 167 BC. After the death of Alexander the Great, Alexander's empire was broken into pieces. One of these pieces was the Seleucid Empire, which controlled what today are Syria, Iran, Iraq, and Israel. When Antiochus Epiphanes became king, he tried to force the Jews to adopt Greek culture and religion. Some were agreeable, but others resisted. Antiochus had a statue of the Greek god Zeus built beside the temple, and he sacrificed a pig on the altar. As Jews consider pigs "unclean", this was extremely offensive. It caused a revolt led by a family called the Maccabees, which means "hammer", because they hammered the Seleucids. The Maccabees created an independent Jewish nation that lasted from about 140 BC until they were conquered by the Romans in 63 BC. The Maccabean family continued as puppet rulers under the Romans until the Romans switched their support to Herod and made him king in 37 BC. (The history of Israel under the Maccabees is fairly complicated: sometimes they were totally independent and sometimes they had varying amounts of local authority under powerful empires. So it's hard to say exactly when they were "independent".)

Side note: Antiochus IV called himself "Epiphanes", the Greek word for "someone who reveals", because he claimed to be the revelation of the Greek god Zeus to mortal men. The Jews called him "Epimenes", which means "the insane person". In

Greek, "epiphanes" and "epimenes" rhyme (ee-PIF-ah-nees and ee-PIM-ah-nees), so it was a joke – they were making fun of his name.

This theory fits, or seems to fit, Daniel 11 very well. Daniel 11 matches what secular historians tell us about the conflict between the Seleucids and the Ptolemies.

But Daniel 9 says that the Abomination of Desolation happens *after* the coming of the Messiah, and in Matthew 24 Jesus refers to it as a future event. Jesus cannot be prophesying about Antiochus, because Antiochus was 200 years before Jesus. Jesus may be saying that this future event will be similar to what Antiochus did.

Many commentators therefore conclude that Daniel is talking about two different events using the same name: Daniel 11 refers to Antiochus; and Daniel 9, as well as Matthew 24, refers to some other, similar event to occur later in history.

Theory 2: Caligula, AD 40. The Roman emperor Caligula ordered the Jews to set up a statue of himself in their temple, to be worshipped as a god. Not surprisingly, the Jews refused. The Roman governor of the province, Petronius, not wanting to ignite a civil war, tried to negotiate a compromise. He sent a letter to Caligula urging him to reconsider. Caligula was furious at the letter and sent a reply ordering Petronius to commit suicide. This was a fairly common option given to upper class people in ancient Rome as an alternative to being executed. Fortunately for the Jews, Caligula was assassinated by his own guards soon after this. (His assassination had nothing to do with the Jews.) Fortunately for Petronius, news of Caligula's death reached him before Caligula's order to commit suicide. Communications in those days were very slow and unreliable. They didn't have telephones or the Internet, of course. A letter could take weeks or months to get from Rome to a place like Judea on the fringes of the empire. It was not uncommon for messages to be received out of order. So Petronius just conveniently ignored the suicide order. The emperor who followed Caligula, Claudius, didn't care about having a statue of Caligula placed in the Jewish temple – Claudius had no great love for Caligula. So he just dropped the matter.

Irrelevant but possibly amusing side note: "Caligula" wasn't his real name, but a nickname. His real name was Gaius Caesar Germanicus. When he was a little boy, his father often brought him along when campaigning with the army. He even had a little soldier's uniform made for him. The soldiers loved the cute little boy in an army uniform. In Latin, they add "-ula" to a word to mean "small" or "having to do with a child". Like in English we sometimes add "-y", like "dog" becomes "doggy", etc. The Latin word for army boots is "caliga", so the soldiers called him "caligula" – "little army boots". He apparently liked the nickname because he continued to use it as an adult.

The main argument against Caligula being the fulfillment of the prophecy is that he never actually defiled the temple. He tried to defile the temple, he ordered his governor and his soldiers to defile the temple, but they never actually did it. Both Daniel and Matthew seem to be describing an event that would actually happen, not just be threatened.

Theory 3: Titus, AD 70. In AD 66, the Jews rebelled against Rome. The Romans responded by sending an army that fought a brutal seven-year war to crush the revolt. Half-way through the war, in AD 70, the Romans, under the leadership of Titus, captured Jerusalem. Titus order the temple destroyed.

In Matthew 24, the disciples called Jesus's attention to the magnificent buildings of the temple. He replied, "Assuredly, I say to you, not one stone shall be left here upon another, that shall not be thrown down." This was literally fulfilled about 40 years later when the Romans destroyed the temple. They set it on fire. The temple was covered with gold, and the fire melted the gold. So the soldiers tore apart the stones so they could loot all the gold.

A catch to this theory is that Titus's destruction of the temple does not quite fit the wording of the prophecy. Jesus said that they would see the Abomination of Desolation "standing in the holy place". But Titus did not put anything in the temple, either an idol or an unclean sacrifice or anything else. He burned it and demolished it.

Advocates of this theory say that Titus certainly did do a vile thing and certainly did leave the temple desolate.

Side note: The Roman historian Suetonius wrote about the lives of Titus and his father, Vespasian, who also spent time in Judea.

> An ancient superstition was current in the East, that out of Judaea would come the rulers of the world. This prediction, as it later proved, referred to two Roman Emperors, Vespasian and his son Titus; but the rebellious Jews, who read it as referring to themselves, murdered their Procurator, routed the Governor-general of Syria when he came down to restore order, and captured an Eagle.
>
> — Suetonius, *Lives of the Twelve Caesars*

(The reference to the "eagle" is this: Roman legions carried a silver or bronze eagle on a tall pole as a standard that the soldiers could rally around in the confusion of battle. It also came to be seen as a ceremonial symbol of the legion. It was considered a disgrace for a legion's eagle to be captured by the enemy. In one case the Romans spent ten years trying to recapture an eagle that was lost in a battle with German tribes.)

When Suetonius read the prophecies about the Messiah coming from Israel, he concluded that it was about these two Roman emperors who had served as governors of Judea before becoming emperor!

Vespasian and Titus did not fit the prophecies. Neither was born in Bethlehem, neither was born to a virgin, neither was descended from David, neither was crucified (they both died of natural causes), etc.

Still, it's interesting that the Romans were aware of prophecies about a coming messiah and took them seriously.

Theory 4: Hadrian, AD 135. After the Jews were defeated in the AD 66 revolt, they tried again in AD 132 under the leadership of Simon Bar Kokhba. They lost again. In AD 135 Emperor Hadrian razed Jerusalem to the ground and built a temple to the Greek god Zeus on the site where the Jewish temple had stood.

Theory 5: The Antichrist, sometime in the future. By this theory, in the future the Jews will rebuild the temple in Jerusalem. Then during the Tribulation the Antichrist will set up a statue of himself in this temple and demand that the Jews worship him. The basic idea behind this scenario is that there will be two Abominations of Desolation: the first by Antiochus, and the second by the Antichrist. By this theory, Jesus was saying, in essence, "Remember Antiochus? When the Antichrist comes, it will be like that again."

Revelation tells us that the False Prophet (section 6.25) sets up an image of the Beast (section 6.19) and orders people to worship it.

> Revelation 13:14-15 And he [the False Prophet] deceives those who dwell on the earth by those signs which he was granted to do in the sight of the beast, telling those who dwell on the earth to make an image to the beast who was wounded by the sword and lived. He was granted *power* to give breath to the image of the beast, that the image of the beast should both speak and cause as many as would not worship the image of the beast to be killed.

Revelation doesn't say that this image is in the Jewish temple, so it may or may not have anything to do with the Abomination of Desolation.

This sounds a great deal like something we are told about the Man of Lawlessness (section 6.21).

> 1 Thessalonians 2:3-4. Let no one deceive you by any means; for *that Day will not come* unless the falling away comes first, and the man of sin is revealed, the son of perdition, who opposes and exalts himself above all that is called God or that is worshiped, so

that he sits as God in the temple of God, showing himself that he is God.

Theory 6: Jesus, AD 34. A totally different theory is that the Abomination of Desolation was the crucifixion of Jesus. Killing Jesus was an abomination. What is made desolate is not the temple but the nation. Daniel's reference to ending the daily sacrifice means not that a tyrant stops the Jews from performing the Old Testament sacrifices, but that Christ's death makes them no longer necessary.

Theory 7: Here's a tentative suggestion that I put forward. I haven't seen this suggested by others: Dome of the Rock, AD 691. Muslims conquered Jerusalem in AD 638. In AD 691 Caliph Abd al-Malik built the Dome of the Rock on the spot where Muslims believe Abraham had been prepared to sacrifice his son Isaac to God. See Genesis 22. This is also the place where the Jewish temple had previously stood.

The Dome of the Rock stands there to this day. Many Jews want to rebuild the temple. But it is generally believed that if it is rebuilt, it must be on the original spot, and they can't do that as long as the Dome of the Rock stands there. Even though Israel now controls the land, they are not prepared to demolish someone else's holy place.

There are tunnels underneath Jerusalem, and I have stood in a small underground room which I am told is the closest you can get to the spot where the Ark of the Covenant stood in the Holy of Holies in the temple.

If Antiochus Epiphanes was the original abomination of desolation because he put an object of worship to Zeus, a false god, in the Jewish temple, perhaps the Dome of the Rock is the second abomination of desolation because it also puts an object of worship to a false god at the site of the Jewish temple.

A catch to this theory is that the Dome of the Rock has stood there for over 1300 years.

6.3. 70 Weeks

Daniel 9:24-27. Seventy weeks are determined for your people and for your holy city, to finish the transgression, to make an end of sins, to make reconciliation for iniquity, to bring in everlasting righteousness, to seal up vision and prophecy, and to anoint the Most Holy. Know therefore and understand, that from the going forth of the command to restore and build Jerusalem until Messiah the Prince, there shall be seven weeks and sixty-two weeks; the street shall be built again, and the wall, even in troublesome times. And after the sixty-two weeks Messiah shall be cut off, but not for Himself; and the people of the prince who is to come shall destroy the city and the sanctuary. The end of it shall be with a flood, and till the end of the war desolations are determined. Then he shall confirm a covenant with many for one week; but in the middle of the week he shall bring an end to sacrifice and offering. And on the wing of abominations shall be one who makes desolate, even until the consummation, which is determined, is poured out on the desolate.

The Hebrew word translated "week" is שבע, pronounced "shib-aw". It means seven of something. When used by itself, it usually means seven days, but it can mean seven of anything. Like, I suppose, the English word "couple" means two of something. If you say just, "a couple", that's usually understood to mean two people in a romantic relationship. But if you say, for example, "a couple of oranges", you mean two oranges. It can be used for two of anything. In the same way, a shib-aw somethings means seven of something, but just "a shib-aw" normally means seven days.

For example, consider this verse. In the original Hebrew, the word shib-aw is used twice. I'll put the two uses in italics.

Genesis 29:27. Fulfill her *week*, and we will give you this one also for the service which you will serve with me still another *seven* years.

The first shib-aw is translated "week" and means a period of seven days. The second shib-aw is translated simply "seven", and it is followed by the word "years" and so is talking about seven years.

Most scholars believe that Daniel is using shib-aw to mean a period of seven years. Mostly because this results in the prophecy making sense, as we shall see.

Daniel says there will be 70 weeks, which he divides into 7, 62, and 1.

The significance of dividing the first 69 weeks into 7 and 62 is not spelled out. Note Daniel says "there shall be 7 weeks and 62 weeks" with no further explanation of what happens during one period and not the other.

He does specifically spell out that it is 69 weeks (7+62) from the command to rebuild Jerusalem until the coming of the Messiah. Then there is a final week when "he shall confirm a covenant with many", but in the middle of that week "he" brings on the Abomination of Desolation (section 6.2).

There are (at least) two mysteries about the timing here:

1. When do the first two periods begin and end? This turns out to be the easier question because this prophecy has already been fulfilled. Nevertheless, there are some rough points on the interpretation.

2. When does the third period begin and end?

Assuming Daniel means "weeks of years", then 69 "weeks" means 69 x 7 = 483 years.

Presumably "Messiah" refers to Jesus Christ.

After the Persians conquered Babylon, in 535 BC Cyrus of Persia made a decree allowing the Jews to rebuild the temple. We know about this from both Babylonian histories and from the book of Ezra in the Bible. Adding 483 years to Cyrus's decree takes us to 52 BC. This is decades before Jesus was born, so it doesn't add up. Also, the prophecy says "restore and build Jerusalem", which appears to mean the city, not just the temple. So for several reasons, Cyrus's decree doesn't fit the prophecy.

Several other kings came and went, and in 457 BC Artaxerxes decreed that the Jews could rebuild the city. See the book of Nehemiah. In those days a key part of a city was the city wall. Of course the primary reason for having a wall was to defend against attack. It also defined the boundaries of the city, and a good wall was a token of prestige, like modern Americans will brag about their city's great sports stadium or tall buildings. But people who opposed the Jews told Artaxerxes that the Jews were rebuilding the city wall because they planned to rebel, and so he put a stop to the rebuilding while he investigated. He was in the middle of a war so this was not his top priority. After the war, he finally got around to this issue, concluded that the Jews were not planning a rebellion, and in 445 BC issued a second decree allowed the rebuilding to continue.

Adding 483 years to Artaxerxes's first decree gives AD 27. Adding 483 years to Artaxerxes's second decree gives AD 39. Both are at least in the general ballpark of Jesus's lifespan.

Some tinker with the calendar to say that the dates come out right to the exact day.

There have been many calendars in use at various times in history, and they don't all have the exact same length for a year.

The Julian calendar used by the Romans had 365 days with a leap day added every fourth year.

Our modern Gregorian calendar has 365 days with a leap day added every fourth year, unless the year is multiple of 100 in which case it's not a leap year, unless it's also a multiple of 400 in which case it is a leap year. (For example 1996 was a leap year. 1700, 1800, and 1900 were not, but 2000 was.)

The Jewish calendar, then and now, is 354 days on regular, non-leap years, with alternating 30 and 29 day months. A leap month of 30 days is added between the 11th and 12th month in 7 out of every 19 years, on years 3, 6, 8, 11, 14, 17, and 19 of the cycle. The modern Jewish calendar has a complex formula for adding or subtracting one day from some years to make Rosh Hashanah ("Jewish New Year") fall on a New Moon, and to prevent Yom Kippur from falling on a Friday or a Sunday, i.e. the day before or after a Sabbath. (Jews are not supposed to work on either Yom Kippur or the Sabbath, and are supposed to make certain preparations for these days the day before. But if the day before is also a non-work day, then you can't do the preparations, creating a problem.) Historians debate just when these rules were added, and just how these issues were handled before.

The Babylonian calendar was similar to the Jewish calendar in that they also had 12 months to a year with leap months added on the same 19 year cycle. But their months did not have a fixed number of days per month. Also, in year 17 of the 19 year cycle, they added the extra month at a different time of year. (The Babylonians, Jews, and Greeks all claim to have invented the 19-year cycle.)

The Egyptian calendar had 12 months of 30 days each with 5 days at the end of the year not considered part of any month, with a 6th extra day added when astronomical observations indicated it was needed.

And so on. So what calendar was Daniel using?

One calculation I've seen goes like this:

Daniel was using (they assert) a "prophetic year" of exactly 360 days. So when Daniel said 69 weeks of years, he meant 69 x 7 x 360 days = 173,880 days.

The Julian calendar has an average of 365.25 days per year. So dividing 173,880 by 365.25 gives 476 years with 21 days left over.

Nehemiah says that Artaxerxes decree was issued in the month of Nisan. If we assume the first of Nisan, this means March 14, 445 BC. Adding 476 years to this gives March 14, AD 32. Then add 21 more days gives April 4, AD 32.

And April 4, AD 32 was the date of Jesus triumphal entry into Jerusalem! So the prophecy is correct to the exact day!

This sounds very impressive, but personally I find it unconvincing for one simple reason: I have seen several similar calculations that, with slightly different assumptions, start and/or end on different dates. But all claim to be accurate to the exact day. Many use some tortured math. For example I saw one that counted from January 1 of the year of Artaxerxes decree with a quick line about "counting inclusively", then going back and adding and subtracting days for various adjustments. That is, at one point they "round off" to the whole year, but then at other points they count specific days in the year, to arrive at a final date that you could never have gotten by either consistently counting whole years or consistently counting days.

No one knows the exact date of Artaxerxes's decree or of Jesus's triumphal entry, so if a calculation doesn't add up by a few days, you can simply shift the claimed dates.

And perhaps the most crucial question: Who says a "prophetic year" is 360 days?

Nowhere does the Bible say that a "prophetic year" is 360 days. Advocates of this theory tend to argue from several proof texts:

Genesis 7:11 says that Noah's Flood began on the 17th day of the 2nd month. Genesis 8:3 says that the Flood lasted 150 days. Genesis 8:4 says the ark came to rest on the 17th day of the 7th month. Therefore, 5 months = 150 days, there are 30 days per month, and a year must then be 12 x 30 = 360 days.

Esther 1:4 says that Ahasuerus had a party that lasted for 180 days. If 6 months = 180 days, then a year must be 360 days.

Revelation 11:2 mentions a period of 42 months, and then 11:3 says 1260 days. 1260 / 42 = 30, so each day is 30 months, 30 x 12 = 360.

But there are many catches to this argument.

The reference to Esther is easiest to dispose of: The Bible says that the party lasted 180 days. Nowhere does it say that this was 6 months. And the length of the party was planned by Ahasuerus, king of Persia. He would surely have used the Persian calendar. It is difficult to imagine why a king of Persia would plan events to match a mystical Jewish "prophetic calendar" for an event that didn't have anything to do with Jews. That's like supposing that the president of the United States would schedule cabinet meetings based on a calendar from an ancient Chinese legend.

The reference to Noah assumes that if 5 months = 150 days that that must mean that all months are exactly 30 days. But there's no reason to assume this. On our modern Gregorian calendar, the same span of dates, the 17th day of the 2nd month to the 17th day of the 7th month is also exactly 150 days: Feb 17 to Mar 17 is 28 days, Mar 17 to Apr 17 is 31, Apr 17 to May 17 is 30, May 17 to Jun 17 is 31, Jun 17 to Jul 17 is 30. 28 + 31 + 30 + 31 + 30 = 150. But our months are not all exactly 30 days. If you took the 6 months from 2/17 to 8/17 you would find that that is 181 days. Dividing by 6 does not give exactly 30. Was this also true of the calendar that Noah used? There's no way to know.

Even if we accepted the 30-day assumption, you can't assume that all years are exactly 12 months and that every year is the same. Calendars then and now often have different numbers of days in different months. They sometimes have different number of days in the same month in different years. Some calendars have days that are not considered part of any month. Most calendars have some provision for leap years.

So even if Noah used a calendar with exactly 30 days per month, we don't know if his year was exactly 12 months. It is quite plausible that if Noah used a fixed 30 day month that he had leap months every few years, or tacked a few extra days onto the end of the year.

The reference to Revelation makes two debatable assumptions: One, it supposes that the 42 months and the 1260 days refer to the same period of time. This is not at all clear from the text. It says that the temple will be given to the Gentiles for 42 months, and in the next verse it says that the Two Witnesses will preach for 1260 days. This might mean that they are preaching during the time that the Gentiles control the temple. Or it might mean that the Gentiles control the temple for 42 months, and then when that's over the Two Witnesses preach for 1260 days. Or the periods may overlap.

Two, even if they are the same period, the argument supposes that there is no rounding. If you read in a history book that some event, a war for example, "lasted 6 months", and you find that it began on March 3, would you understand that to mean that it must have ended on exactly September 3? If you later found that in fact it ended on September 4, would you say that the writer was lying or mistaken when he said it lasted 6 months? What if the war started at 3:15 pm on March 3, and ended at 5:25 pm on September 3? Would you say that he is wrong in saying that it lasted 6 months, because it was really 6 months, 2 hours, and 10 minutes? Surely not. When someone says that an event lasted for some number of months, we don't normally suppose that he means exactly to the microsecond, or even exactly to the day, unless he actually says so. Using the Julian calendar, if an event took 1260 days, depending on just which month it started and whether there's a leap year in there, that would mean about 41 months and 15 days. As that's a period spanning 42 calendar months and that would round off to 42 months, we would very likely refer to that as "42 months".

So I'm not convinced that there is any "prophetic year" of 360 days.

All that said, a number of ancient civilizations used 360 day calendars. The Mayans used a 360 day calendar. The Egyptians may have used a 360 day calendar for some period of time and later added 5 extra days that were not considered part of any month. It appears that several civilizations in the Middle East changed from 360 day calendars to 365 day calendars in the 8th century BC. I am not an expert on this and I am unable to draw conclusions from the evidence I have seen.

Some Christians speculate from this that the year used to be 360 days, but at some point changed to be 365 days. Some theorize that this happened during the Flood. Others say it happened when God made the Sun move backwards (Isaiah 38:4-8) – which happened in the 8th century BC.

There are two ways this could happen physically: one would be for the Earth to take longer to go around the Sun, i.e. for the Earth to move to a different orbit. The other would be for the day to become shorter, i.e. for a year to still be the same number of minutes, but for a day to be about 20 minutes shorter, so that there would then be several more days in a year.

For either thing to happen involves major physics challenges, but then, presumably a God capable of creating the universe could make it happen.

Alternatively, the change may have had nothing to do with astronomical changes, but rather with people inventing better ways to keep their calendar synchronized with the seasons. It was common in ancient times to add leap days or leap months to a year on an irregular schedule, whenever people noticed that the seasons were no longer starting in the same month.

Regardless, if the length of the year has changed, by all accounts this happened before Daniel, so it's not clear how this would apply to interpretation of Daniel's prophecy, or to dates in Revelation. Why would Daniel, writing in 530 BC and talking about events to happen hundreds of years in the future, use a calendar that was obsolete hundreds or thousands of years before he was born? I suppose one could say that he did so because this was the original calendar of Adam and Eve and so was "traditional" or "sacred", even if it was no longer accurate.

In his book *Observations upon the Prophecies of Daniel and the Apocalypse of St. John*, the famous scientist and mathematician Isaac Newton had a different interpretation of the 70 weeks. He understood it to be saying that there would be 70 weeks from the order to rebuild Jerusalem until the death of the Messiah. So adding 70 x 7 = 490 years to 457 BC comes to AD 34, which Newton had previously calculated as the year of Jesus's crucifixion. Thus he considered the numbers to add up to at least within a year. (page 131)

Earlier I mentioned that time periods are not necessarily exact. Newton also makes this point. How precise do we presume the numbers must be? When scientists give measurements, the general assumption, unless specified otherwise, is that the number given is accurate plus or minus ½ of the last digit. That is, if you say, for example, that your beaker contains 127 grams of sodium, other scientists understand this to mean that it is somewhere between 126.5 and 127.5.

So a little later in the chapter on the 70 weeks, while doing some other calculation, Newton discusses different theories about dates in Jesus life and then says that even if you take an early date, it "will fall in the latter part of the last week, which is enough" (page 135). That is, he says that if we're giving dates as "weeks of years", then the "rounding error" could be as large as half a week, i.e. 3 ½ years.

If the dates really do add up exact to the day, that's interesting and impressive, and I don't doubt that an omnipotent God could make that happen. But if the numbers add up to within a year or two, I'd call that a "hit". Given that we don't know many dates in ancient history all that accurately, even if the numbers do add up exact to the day, we can't prove it and most likely wouldn't even know it.

Jesus lived for 30 to 40 years, so if the prophecy is intended to be precise, we could ask, Just what event in Jesus's life is the "end point"? Events that have been proposed include his birth, his baptism by John, the triumphal entry into Jerusalem, his crucifixion, and his resurrection. As the prophecy says "after the sixty-two weeks Messiah shall be cut off", I think the most likely event is his crucifixion.

So putting this all together, the primary theories are:

Theory 1. There are 69 weeks from Artaxerxes first decree to some event early in Jesus's ministry, such as his baptism by John. 457 BC + 483 = AD 27. This is a little early: Jesus baptism and the beginning of his ministry probably weren't until AD 29. Perhaps the prophecy is rounding off; perhaps historians are off a little on the dates. But it's very close.

Theory 2. There are 69 weeks from Artaxerxes second decree to Jesus triumphal entry, or perhaps to the crucifixion, but Daniel is using a calendar with 360 days per year. See the calculations earlier in this chapter. I doubt this theory because I find it too contrived, but I can't rule it out.

Theory 3. There are 70 weeks from Artaxerxes first decree

to the crucifixion. 457 BC + 490 = AD 34. This theory seems to strain the words of the prophecy, but the numbers add up so well that it's hard to dismiss.

The third time span in the prophecy is the final week, often called "Daniel's 70th week". Recall that Daniel says:

> Then he shall confirm a covenant with many for one week; but in the middle of the week he shall bring an end to sacrifice and offering. And on the wing of abominations shall be one who makes desolate, even until the consummation, which is determined, is poured out on the desolate.

There are three main theories about the meaning of the 70th week, which I will call the "big gap", "little gap", and "no gap". (These terms are my invention for this book: I don't know any widely accepted names for these three theories.)

Theory 1: Big gap. This is the most popular theory among Evangelicals. By this theory, the 70th week is a time still in our future. It is the same period that Revelation refers to as the Great Tribulation. That is, the 69th week ends with the coming of Christ, then there is a gap, and the 70th week will come sometime in the future. As Jesus came over 2000 years ago, this gap is at least 2000 years.

Under the big gap theory, the prince who is to come is a future Antichrist. When he makes a covenant for one week, this means the Antichrist makes a treaty with Israel. Under this treaty Israel is able to rebuild the temple and resume the Old Testament sacrifices. But after 3 ½ years he breaks the treaty and stops the sacrifices. Then he sets up a statue of himself in the temple and demands that people worship him. This is the Abomination of Desolation.

Theory 2: Little gap. This is advocated by some Preterists. This theory says that the 69th week ended with Jesus baptism, circa AD 29. The 70th week then began immediately. The first half of the 70th week was the time of Jesus ministry – 3 ½ years.

The prince who is to come is Jesus. When it says he "confirms the covenant", that means he confirms the covenant that God made with Israel during the time of Moses. After the first half of the week, he brings an end to the sacrifice through his death and resurrection. The animal sacrifices are no longer needed because Jesus has become the perfect sacrifice. The first half of the 70th week thus ends about AD 32 or 33 with the crucifixion. Then there is a small gap of about 40 years. In AD 66 the war with Rome begins. 3 ½ years later, Jerusalem falls and the temple is destroyed, making the second half of the 70th week.

A catch to this theory is that the Jewish War didn't end with the fall of Jerusalem: it went on for another 3 ½ years before Israel was finally defeated. It seems to me that an obvious variation on this theory would be to say that the Jewish War is the 70th week. It fits rather neatly: It last 7 years, and half-way through it, at the 3 ½ year mark, Jerusalem is conquered, the temple is destroyed, and the sacrifices end. So the 69 weeks end with the coming of Christ, then there is a small gap of about 40 years, and then the Jewish War is the 70th week. This variation seems more logical to me, but I've never heard anyone else offer it. I just made it up.

Theory 3: No gap. This is also a Preterist theory. Like the little gap theory, it says the 69 weeks ends with Jesus's baptism, and the first half of the 70th week ends with his crucifixion. But by the no gap theory, the second half of the 70th week then begins immediately. It ends with the baptism of Cornelius about AD 35. See Acts 10:1-15. This marks the opening of the Gospel to gentiles.

There are problems with all these theories.

Preterist theories generally note that Daniel talks about half a week of years, i.e. 3 ½ years, and Jesus's ministry lasted about 3 ½ years. But while we know that Jesus's ministry lasted *about* 3 or 4 years, we don't know exactly. It *might* have lasted 3 ½ years. Even if so, that's interesting, but it's hard to see how to make it fit. Daniel says that after 69 weeks the "Messiah shall be cut off". That sounds like the crucifixion, not his baptism or some other event at or near the beginning of his ministry. If the 69th week ends with the crucifixion, then his ministry ends with the 69th week, not half way through the 70th week.

Any no-gap theory struggles to find some event to put at the end of the 70th week. Whether we put the crucifixion at the beginning or the middle of the 70th week, we have to find another significant event to put within the next seven years. There simply is no obvious event. The baptism of Cornelius has been suggested, but nothing in Daniel appears to refer to such an event, and we don't know exactly when that happened.

A general comment applies here. Commentators trying to fit historical events to prophecies will sometimes take an event where the date is uncertain, assume that it must have happened on a date that fits their theory, and then use this date to prove their theory. That is, they determine the date based on the theory, and then "prove" the theory based on the date.

Similarly, it's interesting that the Jewish War, that ended with the destruction of Jerusalem and the temple, lasted 7 years, and that it was 3 ½ years from the start of the war to the destruction of the temple. But again, it's difficult to see exactly how to make the pieces fit.

Any theory that posits a gap has another problem: The whole point of the prophecy appears to be to give a timeline. If there are gaps in the middle, then there is no timeline. Supposing a 2000 year gap seems quite a stretch.

Maybe a case could be made for a small gap. Daniel says, "after the sixty-two weeks Messiah shall be cut off, but not for Himself; and the people of the prince who is to come shall destroy the city and the sanctuary." He seems to lump the crucifixion and the destruction of Jerusalem together. This could mean that the 69 weeks ends with a period that spans from the crucifixion circa AD 34 to the destruction of Jerusalem in AD 70. That is, one could argue that the 69th week ends with a period of 30 or 40 years, and then the 70th week begins.

The first 69 weeks of the prophecy works so well, it was

so clearly and directly fulfilled. But the 70th week is hard to place.

6.4.   Great Tribulation

There are a number of places in the Bible that refer to periods of tribulation. Jews and Christians have certainly been persecuted throughout history. The phrase "great tribulation" shows up three times. (Matthew 24, Mark 13, and Luke 21 appear to be three accounts of the same sermon, so I'm calling them one place.)

> Matthew 24:15-22. "Therefore when you see the 'abomination of desolation,' spoken of by Daniel the prophet, standing in the holy place" (whoever reads, let him understand), "then let those who are in Judea flee to the mountains. Let him who is on the housetop not go down to take anything out of his house. And let him who is in the field not go back to get his clothes. But woe to those who are pregnant and to those who are nursing babies in those days! And pray that your flight may not be in winter or on the Sabbath. For then there will be great tribulation, such as has not been since the beginning of the world until this time, no, nor ever shall be. And unless those days were shortened, no flesh would be saved; but for the elect's sake those days will be shortened.

> Mark 13:14-20. (essentially the same as Matthew 24)

> Luke 21:20-24. (also similar to Matthew 24)

(Note: I'm only quoting a small excerpt from Matthew 24 here. I encourage you to read the whole chapter to get the full picture.)

> Revelation 2:18-22. And to the angel of the church in Thyatira write, These things says the Son of God, who has eyes like a flame of fire, and His feet like fine brass: I know your works, love, service, faith, and your patience; and as for your works, the last are more than the first. Nevertheless I have a few things against you, because you allow that woman Jezebel, who calls herself a prophetess, to teach and seduce My servants to commit sexual immorality and eat things sacrificed to idols. And I gave her time

to repent of her sexual immorality, and she did not repent. Indeed I will cast her into a sickbed, and those who commit adultery with her into great tribulation, unless they repent of their deeds.

Revelation 7:9-17. After these things I looked, and behold, a great multitude which no one could number, of all nations, tribes, peoples, and tongues, standing before the throne and before the Lamb, clothed with white robes, with palm branches in their hands, and crying out with a loud voice, saying, "Salvation belongs to our God who sits on the throne, and to the Lamb!" All the angels stood around the throne and the elders and the four living creatures, and fell on their faces before the throne and worshiped God, saying: "Amen! Blessing and glory and wisdom, Thanksgiving and honor and power and might, Be to our God forever and ever. Amen." Then one of the elders answered, saying to me, "Who are these arrayed in white robes, and where did they come from?" And I said to him, "Sir, you know." So he said to me, "These are the ones who come out of the great tribulation, and washed their robes and made them white in the blood of the Lamb. Therefore they are before the throne of God, and serve Him day and night in His temple. And He who sits on the throne will dwell among them. They shall neither hunger anymore nor thirst anymore; the sun shall not strike them, nor any heat; for the Lamb who is in the midst of the throne will shepherd them and lead them to living fountains of waters. And God will wipe away every tear from their eyes."

Just because all three use the same words doesn't mean they're talking about the same event. (It is the same phrase in Greek as well as in English – ΘΛΙΨΙC ΜΕΓΑΛΗ, thlipsis megalee. "Megalee" means great or big. "Thlipsis" means trouble or persecution.)

There are several other references in prophecy to periods of tribulation that some connect to the Great Tribulation.

Daniel 9:27. Then he shall confirm a covenant with many for one week; But in the middle of the week He shall bring an end to sacrifice and offering. And on the wing of abominations shall be one who makes desolate, Even until the consummation, which is determined, Is poured out on the desolate.

Revelation 2:8-10. And to the angel of the church in Smyrna write, These things says the First and the Last, who was dead, and came to life: I know your works, tribulation, and poverty (but you are rich); and I know the blasphemy of those who say they are Jews and are not, but are a synagogue of Satan. Do not fear any of those things which you are about to suffer. Indeed, the devil is about to throw some of you into prison, that you may be tested, and you will have tribulation ten days. Be faithful until death, and I will give you the crown of life.

Revelation 3:7,10. And to the angel of the church in Philadelphia write, 'These things says He who is holy, He who is true, "He who has the key of David, He who opens and no one shuts, and shuts and no one opens" ... Because you have kept My command to persevere, I also will keep you from the hour of trial which shall come upon the whole world, to test those who dwell on the earth.

Christians commonly say that the great tribulation of Revelation lasts for seven years. Yet nowhere does Revelation say that the tribulation is seven years. Christians get this by connecting the tribulation of Revelation to Daniel's 70th week, and then applying the seven years of Daniel to Revelation. This is certainly possible. However, it is not the plain words of scripture but a conclusion based on a debatable identification.

Preterists say that Matthew 24 (and Mark 13 and Luke 21) have already been fulfilled. They say the prophecy is about the destruction of the temple in AD 70. Futurists generally agree that the prophecy was partially fulfilled in AD 70, but say that much of it will not be fulfilled until some future time.

Many elements of the prophecy are fairly general. Jesus says that there will be wars and natural disasters. Believers will be persecuted. False Messiahs will deceive many and found heretical cults. These things all happened in the events leading up to AD 70, but they have happened at other times in history, and it would not be a stretch to suppose that they might happen again in the future.

Other parts of the prophecy are more specific.

Preterists point out that in Matthew 24 and Mark 13, Jesus

begins by talking about the destruction of the temple, and leads from there to a discussion of a period of tribulation. The most natural reading is that he is describing a series of events that will all happen in rapid succession.

Elements of Jesus's description closely match the destruction of the temple by the Romans in AD 70. Most obviously, he says that the temple will be destroyed. He says that "not one stone will be left upon another". When the Romans captured the temple, they set it on fire. The walls were covered with gold, and the fire melted the gold so it dripped down between the rocks. In order to loot all the gold the Romans tore down the walls. So literally, not one stone was left upon another.

The events surrounding the fall of Jerusalem were truly horrifying. The Romans surrounded and besieged the city. Anyone who tried to escape was killed, not by the Romans at first, but by the Jewish soldiers, as "deserters". They refused to allow their bodies to be buried, but left them lying at the gates or roads were they were caught.

At first people trying to escape who were caught by the Romans were robbed but then let go. Then some refugees got the idea of swallowing gold coins to smuggle them past the Roman lines, with the thought that the gold would, let us say, come out the other end some time after they had escaped. A clever plan, until the besieging army figured it out. Then some of the besiegers, especially the Arabs among them, started cutting open any refugees and searching their guts for coins.

Other refugees the Romans crucified, and stood the crosses up where they could be seen from the city. The leaders in the city forced their families to watch their relatives die as a warning against trying to desert.

The Jews within the city broke up into multiple factions which fought each other. One ploy was to burn each other's food supplies. So while the city was under siege, with the Romans blocking any food from being brought in, the defenders destroyed their own food stocks. When the inevitable famine struck, they fought each other for scraps of food. Armed men roamed the city searching for food to steal. If they saw that someone had closed up his doors and windows, they suspected he was hiding food and broke in. If someone looked healthy it was assumed he must be hiding food. People were tortured and killed if food was found in their house, and were tortured worse if no food was found to force them to reveal where it was hidden.

The Romans delayed assaulting the city on the reasoning that the Jews were more effective at killing Jews than the Romans were. (Josephus, *Wars of the Jews*, book 5)

In verse 34, Jesus says, "Assuredly I say to you, this generation will by no means pass away till all these things take place."

Thus, Preterists conclude, this is a prophecy about the destruction of the temple in AD 70. Many details of the prophecy fit. And Jesus specifically says it will happen to "this generation". Jesus was speaking approximately AD 30. Many people present would still have been alive by AD 70. "This generation" would not have been alive much later than that, certainly not 2000 years later.

Futurists reply that some elements of the prophecy do not fit AD 70. Verse 14 says, "And this gospel of the kingdom will be preached in all the world ... and then the end will come." The gospel had not been preached to the whole world by AD 70. There are many parts of the world today that have still not heard the gospel.

Verse 29 describes astronomical events – the Sun will be darkened and stars will fall from Heaven – that don't fit anything that literally happened in AD 70.

Most important, verses 29 and 30 say that "immediately after the tribulation", Jesus will return. Clearly Jesus did not return in AD 70. The world is still here and history continues.

But if the prophecy is about a future Second Coming, how come the beginning sounds so much like AD 70? And how do we reconcile an interpretation that it is about the future with Jesus's statement that "all these things" would happen to "this generation"?

Note the setting in which Jesus delivers the prophecy. In Matthew 24:1-2, Jesus tells his disciples that the temple will be destroyed. In verse 3 they ask, "When will these things be? And what will be the sign of Your coming, and of the end of the age?"

Some Futurists say that to the disciples, the destruction of such an architecturally magnificent and spiritually significant structure as the temple would only be possible if the whole world was ending. And so they ask when these two events will happen – the destruction of the temple and the Second Coming – thinking that they were one. Jesus then answers their question as if the two events were one. That is, he accommodated his answer to the limited understanding of the disciples.

Personally, I have a big problem with this interpretation. Basically it says that Jesus gave an incorrect, or at least very misleading, answer to a question to accommodate the ignorance of his audience. But on other occasions Jesus had no problem telling people that they were making false assumptions. For example, go back just two chapters, to Matthew 22. The Sadducees asked Jesus what they thought was a stumper of a question: If a woman's husband died and she remarried, then which man would be her husband in Heaven? Would she have two husbands? Jesus replied (Matthew 22:29-30), "You are mistaken, not knowing the Scriptures nor the power of God. For in the resurrection they neither marry nor are given in marriage." He didn't try to accommodate his answer to their incorrect assumptions, but pointed out their mistake.

In a larger sense, I have a problem with any such accomodationist interpretation, as it throws all Scripture into question. If God tells us things that aren't true just to avoid confusing us, how can we know whether anything in Scripture is really true or just such an accommodation? I develop computer software for a living. (Writing is just a sideline.) I often have to explain complicated technical things about computers to people who are not computer experts. When I do, I often leave out a lot of technical detail that my audience would not understand. But I don't say things that aren't true.

In some cases, one could say that the reality is so complicated that being both simple and accurate at the same time is a logical impossibility. Like some say that the account of creation in Genesis 1 is vastly over-simplified because the people at that time, with limited scientific knowledge, would not have understood an accurate account. I doubt that. I am usually able to simplify technical computer explanations without being inaccurate. I am a limited human so sometimes I don't see how to do it, but I think God can do it perfectly: he can make statements that leave out all the complexity that his audience would not understand, while still being 100% accurate.

In this case, surely it would have been easy. All Jesus had to do was say, "No, those two things won't happen at the same time, they are thousands of years apart." It's difficult to see why that would have been hard for the disciples to understand.

An argument I consider more plausible is that Jesus is connecting events that will happen thousands of years apart because they are connected in some spiritual sense. The destruction of the temple and the Second Coming do not happen at the same time, but they are closely related in God's plan, and so he describes them as a single event. Like a businessman might say, "We'll produce the metal frames in Mexico and the fabric in China ...", not implying that the two places are close together, but because both contribute to the same final product.

What about all of these things happening to "this generation"? I have heard two Futurists explanations.

One is that by "generation" Jesus does not mean the group of people living at the same time, but rather a species, namely, the human race. He is saying that the human race will not be destroyed before all this happens.

Maybe, but this runs into a simple dictionary problem. The Greek word translated "generation" is "ΓΕΝΕΑ" (genea). It means the group of people living at the same time. It simply doesn't mean "human race". There's a different Greek word for that. In some cases it might be understood to mean the people of a particular place as well as time.

Americans regularly talk about the "baby boom generation", "the post-Vietnam generation", and so on. We mean all the people born within a certain time period. Often we mean all the *Americans* born within a certain time period, not all the people in the world.

The same Greek word is used in Luke 1:50, "And His mercy is on those who fear Him, from generation to generation." This make sense if we understand "generation" to mean people living at one time: God's mercy goes on from one generation to the next. It doesn't make sense if we substitute "human race". You can't go from one human race to another human race.

Or consider Luke 11:30, "For as Jonah became a sign to the Ninevites, so also the Son of Man will be to this generation." If "generation" means "the human race", then this verse is contrasting "the Ninevites" with "the human race". But of course the Ninevites were members of the human race. They weren't aliens.

I cannot find any verse in the Bible that uses the Greek word "genea" where it does not make sense in context to understand it to mean "the people living at this time". There are many verses that don't make sense if you try to read it as "human race". (Of course there are verses where the meaning is not clear from context. You could say that of any word. If I say, "I own a plugh", and you don't know what the word "plugh" means, you could fit almost anything in there. But if I then say, "I changed the oil in my plugh's engine and put air in the tires ", you'd get the idea it must be a car or some sort of vehicle.)

A Futurist theory that I find more plausible is that when Jesus said "this generation" he didn't mean "the generation living at the time I speak these words", but rather was referring to some other generation identified in the prophecy. They point out that in the previous verses, Jesus had been talking about various signs of his coming. Then in verse 33 he says, "So you also, when you see all these things, know that it is near – at the doors." Then in verse 34 he says "This generation will by no means pass away till all these things take place." So some Futurists say that by "this generation", Jesus meant the generation that "see[s] all these things". That is, when all these signs happen, then he will return within one generation. Still, if you concede that even part of the prophecy is about AD 70, you run into a problem trying to put part of it thousands of years later. Jesus said, "this generation will by no means pass away till all these things take place". Even if we can question just what generation that is, you can't say that one generation will see part of it and another generation will see the rest of it. One generation will see all of it.

The statement about the sun being darkened and stars falling from heaven isn't much of a problem for Preterists, for the simple reason that it's not clear what it means. It can easily be read as being symbolic: In Daniel, stars are used as a symbol for nations. This may mean that nations will fall. It may refer to supernatural events, like fallen angels being kicked out of Heaven. If it's Earthly and literal, "the sun will be darkened" could mean an eclipse, or that the sun will be obscured by clouds. Stars falling could refer to meteorites hitting the Earth. (The Greek word translated "star" here is AΣTEP ("aster"), which means any object in space, not just a star like the English word. Planets and meteorites were considered "asters".)

What about Jesus's statement in verse 14 that "this gospel of the kingdom will be preached in all the world"? Even today the gospel has not reached every person in the world. It certainly hadn't by AD 70.

But this is assuming that the word "all" is meant absolutely literally.

Paul begins the Epistle to the Romans by praising them because, verse 8, "your faith is spoken of throughout the whole world". Did Paul mean that literally every human being in the world was aware of the faith of the church in Rome? That people in China and Australia and the Pacific islands and the Americas had heard of them and their faith? Probably not. It is far more likely that he means that many people from many different places have heard of their faith.

Similarly, Paul tells the Colossians (Colossians 1:5-6) that "the gospel, which has come to you, as it has also in all the world ..." Had the gospel really reached "all the world" by the time the Epistle to the Colossians was written circa AD 60? If you say, yes, it had, then Jesus prophecy in Matthew 24 was indeed fulfilled by AD 70. If more realistically you say no, that Paul did not mean literally the whole world, but simply many places in the world, then maybe Jesus meant the same.

The much bigger problem for Preterists is the discussion of Jesus returning. Clearly Jesus did not return in AD 70.

Or did he? Preterists say that when Jesus said he was coming back in Matthew 24, he didn't mean the "Second Coming" as most Christians think of the phrase: coming back in power and glory, so that the whole world sees him and knows he has come back, and then setting up a divine kingdom on Earth. Rather, they say that he "came back" in the sense that he intervened in human history to judge the nation of Israel. In much the same way that God judged Israel in the past by sending the Assyrians and the Babylonians to defeat them in battle, now he was acting to send the Romans. We'll discuss this idea of the Second Coming further in section 6.7

So, in conclusion, there are three basic theories about the timing of the tribulation:

Theory 1. The Great Tribulation has already happened. It was the tribulation surrounding the Jewish War when Israel rebelled against the Romans, climaxing in the fall of Jerusalem and the destruction of the temple in AD 70. It lasted for 7 years, from AD 66 to AD 73. (Preterist theory)

Theory 2. The Great Tribulation is an event still to come. At some future date the Antichrist will come to power, beginning a seven year period when people will suffer under both the tyranny of the Antichrist and the judgement of God. (Futurist theory)

Theory 3. There is no single "great tribulation". It is not "the Great Tribulation" with a capital "T", but rather "a great tribulation". There have been many times of tribulation in the past and there will be more in the future, and some of these are bad enough that they can be described as "great tribulations". (A theory mostly held by Preterists, but consistent with Futurism.)

Are the tribulations of Daniel 7, Matthew 24, and Revelation the same period?

Most Futurists say yes: All three are describing a tribulation to take place at some time in the future.

Most Preterists say that Daniel 7 and Matthew 24 are both about AD 70. Many Preterists say that Revelation is also primarily about AD 70. Some Partial Preterists say that Revelation is about a future tribulation, and therefore not AD 70.

So Futurists and Preterists generally agree that all three are talking about the same time period. They just disagree about when that time is, by at least 2000 years!

Who are the victims of the tribulation?

If the tribulation happened in AD 70, then the victims were the Jews.

Jewish persecution of Christians drove many Christians out of Jerusalem well before this date. A number of historians say that the remainder left before the city was besieged.

For example, Eusebius, in his book, *History of the Church,* written about AD 324, says:

[T]he remaining apostles, in constant danger from murderous plots, were driven out of Judaea. But to teach their message they travelled into every land in the power of Christ, who had said to them: "Go and make disciples of all nations in my name." Furthermore, the members of the Jerusalem church, by means of an oracle given by revelation to acceptable persons there, were ordered to leave the City before the war began and settle in a town in Peraea called Pella.

— Eusebius, *History of the Church,* 3:5.

Josephus notes that early in the war, the Roman general

Cestius withdrew from attacking Jerusalem for no apparent reason.

> It then happened that Cestius was not conscious either how the besieged despaired of success, nor how courageous the people were for him; and so he recalled his soldiers from the place, and by despairing of any expectation of taking it, without having received any disgrace, he retired from the city, without any reason in the world.
>
> – Josephus, *Wars of the Jews*, 19:6:7

Many Christians have suggested that Cestius withdrawal was arranged by God to give Christians a final chance to flee from Jerusalem. So Christians largely escaped the tribulation of AD 70.

If we are talking about a future tribulation, things get murkier.

Most Futurists believe that Christians will be taken out of the world by the Rapture before the Great Tribulation. (See section 6.6.) However, most believe that people will be saved during the Tribulation. Thus, the victims of the Great Tribulation would be Jews and people who convert to Christianity after the Rapture. The unsaved will also suffer greatly during this period.

6.5. Millennium

The Millennium is a period during which Satan is bound and unable to operate, at least nominally 1000 years.

The primary source text for the Millennium is:

Revelation 20:1-4. Then I saw an angel coming down from heaven, having the key to the bottomless pit and a great chain in his hand. He laid hold of the dragon, that serpent of old, who is the Devil and Satan, and bound him for a thousand years; and he cast him into the bottomless pit, and shut him up, and set a seal on him, so that he should deceive the nations no more till the thousand years were finished. But after these things he must be released for a little while. And I saw thrones, and they sat on them, and judgment was committed to them. Then I saw the souls of those who had been beheaded for their witness to Jesus and for the word of God, who had not worshiped the beast or his image, and had not received his mark on their foreheads or on their hands. And they lived and reigned with Christ for a thousand years.

There are several other passages that may be talking about the same period.

Isaiah 2:2-4. Now it shall come to pass in the latter days That the mountain of the Lord's house Shall be established on the top of the mountains, And shall be exalted above the hills; And all nations shall flow to it. Many people shall come and say, "Come, and let us go up to the mountain of the Lord, To the house of the God of Jacob; He will teach us His ways, And we shall walk in His paths." For out of Zion shall go forth the law, And the word of the Lord from Jerusalem. He shall judge between the nations, And rebuke many people; They shall beat their swords into plowshares, And their spears into pruning hooks; Nation shall not lift up sword against nation, Neither shall they learn war anymore.

Isaiah 24:21-23. It shall come to pass in that day That the Lord will punish on high the host of exalted ones, And on the earth the kings of the earth. They will be gathered together, As prisoners are gathered in the pit, And will be shut up in the prison; After many days they will be punished. Then the moon will be disgraced And the sun ashamed; For the Lord of hosts will reign On Mount Zion and in Jerusalem And before His elders, gloriously.

Zechariah 14:9. And the Lord shall be King over all the earth. In that day it shall be — "The Lord is one," And His name one.

(The rest of Zechariah 14 may also relate to the Second Coming.)

Some commentators go in a different direction and instead connect the Millennium to:

Luke 17:20-21. Now when He was asked by the Pharisees when the kingdom of God would come, He answered them and said, "The kingdom of God does not come with observation; nor will they say, 'See here!' or 'See there!' For indeed, the kingdom of God is within you."

The Millennium is a key element in Second Coming prophecy. How one interprets the Millennium affects how one interprets many other events.

There are three basic theories. These are usually classified in terms of where one puts the Millennium in relation to the Second Coming.

Premillennial: The Second Coming happens before the Millennium. Christ returns in a very literal, physical, personal way and rules the Earth for 1000 years.

Premillennialists generally suppose that there will be no ambiguity here. At his first coming, people could plausibly deny that Jesus was the Messiah, and people continue to do so to this day. While Christians argue that there is strong historical evidence to prove that Jesus really did perform miracles and rise from the dead, still, it is not totally absurd or insane for someone to say that he is unconvinced. If he wasn't there to see the miracles, it's not obvious. By the Premillennial theory, this will not be possible during the Millennium. Jesus will come in a way visible to millions, and will rule the world from Jerusalem. If someone questioned if Jesus is really the Messiah, he could just go to Jerusalem and see for himself.

Christ rules the world for 1000 years. During this time, Satan is imprisoned. At the end of the 1000 years, Satan is released for one final battle against God.

Postmillennial: The Gospel spreads around the world, until everyone, or at least a large majority, become Christians. The Church creates a golden age of peace, prosperity, and righteousness. This lasts for 1000 years. At the end of this time, Christ returns to establish his kingdom on Earth.

In some Postmillennial theories, the Millennium does not begin until the golden age is achieved. The Church triumphs over the forces of sin and ignorance, then there is a thousand years of paradise, and finally Christ returns.

In other theories, the Millennium is a period when the spread of the Gospel and the influence of the Church gradually grow. The Millennium does not start as a golden age, but it ends as one. When the world finally reaches the point of universal peace and love, then it is ready for Christ to return. That is, it takes 1000 years from the beginning of this period to the final victory of the Church.

In either case, Postmillennialists say that the Church creates this paradise on Earth. They sometimes use phrases like "make the world ready for Christ's return".

Just to be clear: They're not saying that the Church accomplishes this through human effort. It's not like humans must work very hard to makes themselves worthy of Christ. That would be impossible. We are sinners saved by grace, and we're not going to fix that problem by working really, really hard. The point is that Christ works through the Church to bring this result about, just as throughout the Bible God often worked through human beings. In that sense, Premillennialists say that God brings about the Millennium through direct, supernatural intervention in history. Postmillennialists say that he brings the Millennium through more subtle working through human beings.

In ancient times and the early Middle Ages, many people believed that the Millennium began with Jesus's first coming. If the 1000 years began with his birth, then his Second Coming would be approximately AD 1000.

Saint Augustine (AD 354-430) believed that the world was created in 5350 BC. Thus the sixth millennium, i.e. the sixth thousand-year period of Earth history, began in 350 BC. Augustine theorized that the sixth was the Millennium of Revelation, and so the Millennium would end and Christ would return about AD 650.

When AD 650 came and went with no Second Coming, Augustine was proven wrong. When AD 1000 came and went with no Second Coming, Postmillennialists modified the theory to say that the clock began at his crucifixion or resurrection or perhaps at the Ascension. But even to people who put the latest possible date on his life, by the time 1050 or 1100 rolled around, it was becoming clear that this theory wasn't true.

One option for people who hold this theory today is to say that the 1000 years is not a literal number, but simply means a long period of time. So the Millennium began with Christ's first coming. It's already lasted 2000 years and has an indeterminate amount of time left to go.

Some point to verses like 2 Peter 3:8b, "[W]ith the Lord one day is as a thousand years, and a thousand years as one day." Thus, they say, the 1000 years could be one day; it could be a million years; it could be any amount of time.

In my opinion, this is unlikely. The Bible gives a very specific number: 1000 years. I could accept that this is a round number. If someone had a theory where the length of the Millennium came out to be 997 years, I could accept that the Bible is rounding this off. But to suggest that the Bible says 1000 years, and really means over 2000 years ... why would God have given a number if it bore no relation to the real number?

Let me make a general comment here. People use 2 Peter 3:8 to justify ignoring any statement in the Bible that gives an amount of time so they can then substitute some other amount of time that fits their theory, usually a theory about prophecy or about when the Earth was created. I reject this idea on the most basic principle of interpretation. Not just interpreting the Bible, but interpreting any book. You can't just ignore words that don't fit your pet theories. You can't assume that the author didn't mean what he said and then substitute some totally different meaning that has no relation to the actual words. To get back to this specific example: If God didn't mean 1000 years, why did he say "1000 years"? If he meant "a long unspecified period of time", why didn't he say that? A number could certainly be a round number rather than exact. One could make a case that a number is symbolic. But you can't just ignore the text and substitute what you think God should have said.

The other alternative is to put the start of the Millennium at some date other than the First Coming. Various dates have been proposed. For example, some say the Millennium will begin when everyone on Earth has heard the Gospel. Others have picked some historical event they consider significant. Usually these are dates that later generations quickly find forgettable, like the date that the leader of their denomination was born. In my humble opinion, the beginning of the Protestant Reformation or the date that Israel was re-established would be obvious candidates, and I'm surprised that I haven't read anyone suggesting these. It is certainly possible that there was or will be some pivotal event in history that marks the start of the Millennium. Even if that date is already past, we may not recognize it until much later. Like historians regularly say, "No one realized it at the time, but this event marked the true beginning of World War 2" or some such critical event.

Amillennial: The Millennium is not a literal period of time, but is a symbol or an allegory for the spread of the Gospel.

To my mind, this sounds a lot like those variations of the Postmillennial theory that say that the 1000 years is not literal. By saying it is not literal, it avoids problems about when the Millennium begins or how long it lasts.

It could be said that Premillennialists are essentially pessimists and Postmillennialists are essentially optimists. Premillennialists believe that the world is getting worse and worse, and eventually God will intervene with judgment. Postmillennialists say that the world is getting better and better, and eventually we will reach a golden age.

I presume that any reasonable person on either side would readily concede that there have been ups and downs throughout history. But what is the overall trend?

Every now and then I see a survey where they ask a question like, "Do you think America is headed in the right direction?" How do you answer such a question? At any given time, there are dozens of things that are going well and dozens that are going badly. If salaries are rising but at the same time fewer new jobs are being created, is the economy overall doing well or poorly? Or from a spiritual point of view, as I write this, polls show that more and more Americans oppose abortion, but at the same time more and more Americans support gay marriage. The Christian church in Europe is disappearing under a wave of secularism, but Christianity is growing like wildfire in China and the Middle East. (Statisticians say that if present trends continue, in 10 to 20 years there will be more Christians in China than in the United States. Though we should note that there are many more people in China, so as a percentage of the population they will still be fewer.)

Even if you could prove that by some objective standard, today the world is getting worse, perhaps in 50 years that trend will reverse. Or vice versa if you think that today the world is getting better.

What does it mean when it says that Satan will be bound?

The plain reading is that this is literal: God will lock Satan in some sort of prison. It's not clear what sort of prison is needed to confine a fallen angel. The description here doesn't mention walls or bars, but rather a bottomless pit and a seal.

The other obvious interpretation is that this is figurative. It is not that Satan is literally locked in a prison, but that God limits his actions in some way.

There's also mention of the angel carrying a chain. I don't know anyone who claims the chain is literal, that Satan could be bound with a chain. If the chain is figurative, that is reason to believe that the rest of the description is figurative.

Then the question becomes "how figurative?" Perhaps the actual forces needed to imprison Satan are difficult to describe in terms that humans can understand, so God describes them with the symbol of a chain. By that reasoning Satan being "bound" does not necessarily mean literally tied up, but still, confined in his movements in some way.

For that matter, can we be so sure the chain is not literal?

Maybe we are out-sophisticating ourselves. Maybe Satan can be bound with a chain. Maybe he can be bound with the right kind of chain – a chain with the right sort of energy running through it or some such. Who knows?

I wonder if the "bottomless pit" may mean a black hole, a star whose gravity field is so strong that not even light can escape. Perhaps an angel could not escape from such a place either.

Premillennialists generally theorize that the imprisonment is literal: God locks Satan up for 1000 years while Jesus rules on Earth. Then at the end of this time Satan is released for one last act of rebellion.

Postmillennialists are split. Some say that the spread of the Gospel and the growing influence of the Church erode Satan's power. Fewer and fewer people fall for his tricks and temptations. His power shrinks. Alternatively, the Holy Spirit restrains Satan's actions on Earth.

Others say that it's literal. At some point God will lock Satan up, much like the Premillennialists say. This makes it possible for the world to experience a golden age.

6.6. Rapture

The idea of the Rapture is that Christ will miraculously remove believers from the world and take them to Heaven. Some imagine people floating up into the sky and flying to Heaven. Most picture the believers simply vanishing in an instant.

The idea of the Rapture comes primarily from three passages:

1 Corinthians 15:51-52. Lo! I tell you a mystery. We shall not all sleep, but we shall all be changed, in a moment, in the twinkling of an eye, at the last trumpet. For the trumpet will sound, and the dead will be raised imperishable, and we shall be changed.

Matthew 24:37-41. As were the days of Noah, so will be the coming of the Son of man. For as in those days before the flood they were eating and drinking, marrying and giving in marriage, until the day when Noah entered the ark, and they did not know until the flood came and swept them all away, so will be the coming of the Son of man. Then two men will be in the field; one is taken and one is left. Two women will be grinding at the mill; one is taken and one is left.

1 Thessalonians 4:15-17. For this we declare to you by the word of the Lord, that we who are alive, who are left until the coming of the Lord, shall not precede those who have fallen asleep. For the Lord himself will descend from heaven with a cry of command, with the archangel's call, and with the sound of the trumpet of God. And the dead in Christ will rise first; then we who are alive, who are left, shall be caught up together with them in the clouds to meet the Lord in the air; and so we shall always be with the Lord.

Many find a parallel between the Rapture and two other case of people who, the Bible tells us, were taken directly to Heaven without ever dying.

The first was Enoch. We're not told a lot about Enoch. Besides bare facts like the name of his father (Jared), and a son (Methuselah), all the Bible says about him is:

Genesis 5:24. And Enoch walked with God; and he *was* not, for God took him.

Hebrews 11:5. By faith Enoch was taken away so that he did not see death, and was not found, because God had taken him; for before he was taken he had this testimony, that he pleased God.

Jude 14-15. Now Enoch, the seventh from Adam, prophesied about these men also, saying, "Behold, the Lord comes with ten thousands of His saints, to execute judgment on all, to convict all who are ungodly among them of all their ungodly deeds which they have committed in an ungodly way, and of all the harsh things which ungodly sinners have spoken against Him."

That's it. It's one of those stories in the Bible where few facts are given and we are left to wonder about the rest of the story. (I find it rather maddening but I suppose God has a reason.) The relevant point here is, apparently God took Enoch directly to Heaven. We're not told just how or why God did this.

The second was Elijah. We're told quite a bit about Elijah,

including his being taken up to Heaven. See 2 Kings 2. I won't quote it all here, but the highlight is:

> 2 Kings 2:11-12a. Then it happened, as they [Elijah and Elisha] continued on and talked, that suddenly a chariot of fire *appeared* with horses of fire, and separated the two of them; and Elijah went up by a whirlwind into heaven. And Elisha saw *it,* and he cried out, "My father, my father, the chariot of Israel and its horsemen!" So he saw him no more.

The idea of the Rapture is actually fairly new. It is generally credited to John Darby in 1830. Some question whether Darby thought of it himself or got the idea from someone else. That debate isn't important to our purposes here, so let me just say that if Darby didn't invent it, he made it popular.

The word "rapture" does not appear anywhere in the Bible in reference to such an event. (The word "rapture" does not appear at all in most English translations. It does appear in the Darby version, but, ironically, not to refer to "the Rapture", but in an entirely different context, in Song of Solomon 2:3, "In his shadow have I rapture".)

Of course the fact that the word isn't used in the Bible doesn't mean that the idea is not Biblical. The word "trinity" doesn't appear in the Bible either, but the concept is there. The same could be said for many words used for Christian doctrines.

Likewise, the fact that the theory is relatively new doesn't prove it's false. Prophecies that mention Israel have been re-interpreted since Israel became a nation again in 1948. Etc. Nevertheless, it is fair to be troubled by the fact that it went undiscovered for so long. We have to believe that the apostles Paul and John taught this doctrine, and then that it was misunderstood and forgotten for 1700-plus years before being re-discovered by Mr Darby. Not impossible, but it raises questions.

There are four basic theories about the Rapture. These theories are named based on when the Rapture happens in relation to the Tribulation.

Pre-Tribulation Rapture, or "Pre-trib" for short: The

Rapture comes just before the Tribulation.

Mid-Tribulation Rapture, or "Mid-trib": The Rapture comes in the middle of the Tribulation. Advocates of this theory believe the Tribulation will last 7 years, so the Rapture comes at the 3 ½ year point.

Post-Tribulation Rapture, or "Post-trib": The Rapture comes after the Tribulation.

Arapture: There is no Rapture.

I am an Arapturist. I will try to present the other views fairly here, but you might keep that in mind.

By the Pre-Trib theory, the purpose of the Rapture is to spare the Church from the time of judgement that God is about to bring on the world. Some say that removing the Church from the world removes a barrier to Satan and evil people: with Christians gone, there is little opposition to their schemes.

There are several Biblical arguments made to support this timing.

> 2 Thessalonians 2:3-7. Let no one deceive you by any means; for *that Day will not come* unless the falling away comes first, and the man of sin is revealed, the son of perdition, who opposes and exalts himself above all that is called God or that is worshiped, so that he sits as God in the temple of God, showing himself that he is God. Do you not remember that when I was still with you I told you these things? And now you know what is restraining, that he may be revealed in his own time. For the mystery of lawlessness is already at work; only He who now restrains *will do so* until He is taken out of the way.

The Second Coming cannot happen until the "man of sin", i.e. the "Man of Lawlessness" (see section 6.21) is revealed. And the Man of Lawlessness cannot be revealed until "what is restraining" him is removed. And what could be restraining him except the Holy Spirit, acting through the Church? Therefore, sometime before the Second Coming, there must be a period where the Church is removed from the world.

Revelation 3:10. Because you have kept My command to persevere, I also will keep you from the hour of trial which shall come upon the whole world, to test those who dwell on the earth.

This promise is specifically given to one of the seven churches mentioned in Revelation, the church of Philadelphia. We'll discuss the seven churches more in section 6.17.

Advocates of this theory point out that in Revelation, the Church is discussed in chapters 1 through 3, and then again in chapter 19 and following, but there is no mention of the Church in chapters 4 through 18. They say this is because the Church is raptured at the beginning of chapter 4, and then is not present in the world until Christ returns, bringing believers back to Earth with him, in chapter 19.

One could debate this. Revelation is filled with symbols, and some commentators interpret some of the symbols in these chapters to be references to the Church. Some say the Woman Dressed in the Sun, Revelation 13, section 6.23, is the Church. Some say the Two Witnesses, Revelation 11, section 6.26, are Christian preachers. Etc.

This argument is also considerably weakened, to my mind anyway, by the fact that while the word "church" does not occur, the word "saints" occurs eleven times (5:8, 8:3, 8:4, 11:18, 13:7, 13:10, 14:12, 15:3, 16:6, 17:6, 18:24).

Some Pre-Tribbers say that Revelation 4:1 refers to the Rapture:

Revelation 4:1. After these things I looked, and behold, a door *standing* open in heaven. And the first voice which I heard *was* like a trumpet speaking with me, saying, "Come up here, and I will show you things which must take place after this."

But in context, this is addressed specifically to John, telling him that he is invited to Heaven so that prophecies can be revealed to him. It is something that happened to one man circa AD 100, not to the entire Church at some future time. Some Pre-Tribbers concede this but say that it has a double meaning: It is a direct statement to John in AD 100, but it is also a prophecy about the future.

A key argument for the Pre-Trib position is this:

1 Thessalonians 5:9. For God did not appoint us to wrath, but to obtain salvation through our Lord Jesus Christ.

If Christians are "not appointed to wrath", that must mean that they will not experience God's judgement. Thus, the Church must be removed from the world before God's judgement begins.

Pre-Tribbers point out that there were occasions in the Bible where God rescued believers from a judgement that was coming on others. Perhaps the best examples are Noah and Lot. God sent the flood to destroy the world, but he warned Noah in advance and told him how to escape. Similarly, before destroying Sodom, God warned Lot to escape and sent angels to escort him out. Some include Enoch on such a list: though we are not told why God took Enoch to Heaven, whether it was to protect him from judgement or for some other reason.

On the other hand, throughout history Christians have certainly suffered with the guilty when God has judged nations.

The Bible warns us on a number of occasions that Christians *will* experience tribulation and persecution. For example, in John 16:33 Jesus warns the disciples, "In the world you will have tribulation." In Romans 5:3-4, Paul encourages Christians facing trials: "we also glory in tribulations, knowing that tribulation produces perseverance; and perseverance, character; and character, hope."

Scripture and history both tell us that Christians have often experienced tribulation. It is possible that God will spare Christians from the Great Tribulation. Maybe that's what God meant by 1 Thessalonians 5:9. God did provide an escape for Noah and Lot. He might do the same here.

The Mid-Trib theory is similar to Pre-Trib in its understanding of purpose. It differs in timing.

Again, the purpose of the Rapture is to spare Christians from God's judgment. That part of the argument is generally the same.

Several prophecies that are taken to apply to the Great Tribulation divide the period into two halves.

In Daniel 9, the prophecy of the 70 Weeks, the last week is often taken to be the Great Tribulation. Daniel 9:27 talks about crucial events that happen "in the middle of the week".

Revelation 11:2 says that the Gentiles will "tread the holy city underfoot for 42 months". 42 months is 3 ½ years.

Revelation 12:6 says that the "women dressed in the sun", section 6.23, hides in the wilderness for 1260 days. 1260 days is a few days short of 3 ½ years. It's exactly 3 ½ times 360, so if you accept the theory of a "prophetic year" of 360 days, see section 6.3, it matches exactly.

Mid-Tribbers often say that the first half of the Tribulation is evil brought by men, while the second half is judgment brought by God. So Christians are spared God's judgment, the second half, but not the human evil of the first half.

Mid-Tribbers equate the trumpet of 1 Corinthians 15:52 with the trumpet of Revelation 11:15.

> 1 Corinthians 15:52. … in a moment, in the twinkling of an eye, at the last trumpet. For the trumpet will sound, and the dead will be raised incorruptible, and we shall be changed.

> Revelation 11:15. Then the seventh angel sounded: And there were loud voices in heaven, saying, "The kingdoms of this world have become *the kingdoms* of our Lord and of His Christ, and He shall reign forever and ever!"

The "seventh angel" in Revelation refers to seven angels who blow trumpets to announce a series of judgements. So if there are seven angels with seven trumpets, the "last trumpet" is the seventh. They then place the Seventh Trumpet half-way through the Tribulation.

I think this is possible, but it is unconvincing. First, Corinthians does not say that it is talking about the seven trumpets of Revelation. The "last trumpet" may refer to the last of some other set of trumpets. Or, I would say more likely, it may be a poetic way to say "the end of an era", without any particular series of trumpets in mind, just "the last trumpet of all before the end of the world".

Second, it is not at all clear that the seventh trumpet of Revelation marks the mid-point of the Tribulation. Revelation 11:15 says that at the seventh trumpet, Christ now begins a reign that will last forever. That would seem to indicate that the Tribulation is now over. The seventh trumpet is not the middle, but the end.

Post-Tribbers make exactly this argument to say that the Rapture comes at the end of the Tribulation.

They point to Jesus's discussion of the sequence:

Matthew 24:29-31. Immediately after the tribulation of those days the sun will be darkened, and the moon will not give its light; the stars will fall from heaven, and the powers of the heavens will be shaken. Then the sign of the Son of Man will appear in heaven, and then all the tribes of the earth will mourn, and they will see the Son of Man coming on the clouds of heaven with power and great glory. And He will send His angels with a great sound of a trumpet, and they will gather together His elect from the four winds, from one end of heaven to the other.

Note the sequence: "after the tribulation ...", then Christ returns, and then the Rapture.

Revelation 20:1-5. Then I saw an angel coming down from heaven, having the key to the bottomless pit and a great chain in his hand. He laid hold of the dragon, that serpent of old, who is *the* Devil and Satan, and bound him for a thousand years; ... Then *I saw* the souls of those who had been beheaded for their witness to Jesus and for the word of God, who had not worshiped the beast or his image, and had not received *his* mark on their foreheads or on their hands. And they lived and reigned with Christ for a thousand years. But the rest of the dead did not live again until the thousand years were finished.

Here the sequence is: Satan is bound, Rapture, Millennium. Satan can't be bound until the Tribulation is over, so this indicates that the Rapture happens after the Tribulation.

Post-Tribbers sometimes say that while it would certainly be nice to believe that Christians will not have to go through the Tribulation, we can't make conclusions about what is true based on what would be nice to believe.

Arapturists say that there is no Rapture, and that the verses used to support the idea of a Rapture are being misinterpreted.

Matthew 24 is the easiest to identify as a problem. It is very commonly used as a description of the Rapture, especially the part about "two men will be in the field; one is taken and one is left", etc. Christians have made movies where we see two people working side by side and suddenly one of them disappears, taken up in the Rapture.

Except ... in Matthew, who is "taken"? Read it again: "For as in those days before the flood they were eating and drinking, marrying and giving in marriage, until the day when Noah entered the ark, and they did not know until the flood came and swept them all away, so will be the coming of the Son of man. Then two men will be in the field; one is taken and one is left. Two women will be grinding at the mill; one is taken and one is left." It doesn't say, "and then they got in the ark and were taken away", but "the flood came and swept them all away". It was not Noah and his family who were "taken", but the unbelievers. "Taken" in Matthew 24 does not refer to a miraculous supernatural rescue, but just the opposite: being killed, drowned in the flood.

1 Thessalonians 4:15-17 also has a problem: 1 Thessalonians was written by the apostle Paul about AD 50. Paul died about AD 67. And yet in the book, he says, "we who are alive will be caught up to meet him in the air". *We* who are alive. If you read the original Greek, the "we" is emphatic. If this is referring to a Rapture that is to take place thousands of years after Paul died, how can he say "we who are alive" at this time? Wouldn't he have said "those who are alive"? For a more complete discussion of this, see Second Coming, section 6.7. It

certainly appears that Paul is talking about an event that will occur within his lifetime. I've heard many pro-Rapturists say that Paul simply hoped it would happen in his lifetime. But he doesn't say "I hope I will be alive". His wording implies he *will* be alive. We could say that Paul is just mistaken, of course. But if Paul is wrong about when the Rapture will happen, how do we know he is right about how it will happen, or that it will happen at all? And of course if we say that the Bible is wrong on this point, then we have to throw out the whole idea of the infallibility of scripture.

Arapturists say that most other "Rapture verses" are talking about the Resurrection. 1 Corinthians 15 and 1 Thessalonians 4 both say that the "dead will be raised" and given their new, immortal bodies, and then say that believers still living will also be transformed into immortal bodies at this time.

Earlier I quoted from Revelation 20. This is describing the time when Satan is bound for 1000 years. Let's read a little further.

> Revelation 20:4-6. Then *I saw* the souls of those who had been beheaded for their witness to Jesus and for the word of God, who had not worshiped the beast or his image, and had not received *his* mark on their foreheads or on their hands. And they lived and reigned with Christ for a thousand years. But the rest of the dead did not live again until the thousand years were finished. This *is* the first resurrection. Blessed and holy *is* he who has part in the first resurrection.

So right after Satan is bound, *some* believers are resurrected, the "first resurrection". Then after the 1000 years, "the rest of the dead" are resurrected. The plain reading, then, is that there are two resurrections, no more, no less. There cannot be other resurrections before or after: The resurrection at the start of the 1000 years is "the first", so presumably there can't be any before that. Then he says "the rest" are resurrected at the end of the 1000 years, so there can't be another resurrection after that.

So when 1 Corinthians 15 and 1 Thessalonians 4 talk about believers being resurrected, it must refer to one of these two resurrections. If the living are caught up with the resurrected dead, then any "Rapture" must also happen at this same time.

But the time of the two resurrections is clearly spelled out as being at the beginning and the end of the Millennium. To harmonize a Pre-Trib theory with these verses we would have to say that the Tribulation overlaps the Millennium or comes after the Millennium, which is not what most Pre-Tribbers believe.

Arapturists reject the idea that Revelation 3:10, "I also will keep you from the hour of trial which shall come upon the whole world", means that all believers will be miraculously delivered from the Great Tribulation. It is a prophecy directed to one specific church, the "Church of Philadelphia". Depending on your interpretation of the Seven Churches, section 6.17, the fulfillment may already be passed. Even if we understand these churches to be representatives of types that will exist throughout history, it is not clear that all Christians living at the time of the Great Tribulation will be of the Church of Philadelphia. And there's no particular reason to believe that "keep you from the hour of trial" means being taken out of the world through a Rapture. It could mean that God will provide a place of safety on Earth, or generally will protect believers.

Many Bible verses warn Christians that they will suffer through tribulation. For example:

> Acts 14:22. We must through many tribulations enter the kingdom of God.

> Revelation 2:10. Do not fear any of those things which you are about to suffer. ... you will have tribulation ten days. Be faithful until death, and I will give you the crown of life.

(It seems unlikely that the 10 days is a literal period of time. That would seem too short to be worthy of such special note. Maybe it's a particularly intense 10 days. But we won't get into that here.)

Note there's no Earthly escape from this tribulation: it's "until death".

In the same Matthew 24 sermon used to prove the

Rapture, Jesus says:

Matthew 24:9. Then they will deliver you up to tribulation and kill you, and you will be hated by all nations for My name's sake.

He doesn't say that Christians will be kept safe from the tribulation, but that they will suffer through it.

Thus, the Arapturist concludes, there is no "Rapture". There are two Resurrections, and at one of these Resurrections, the living believers are also given immortal bodies. You can call the gathering of the living saints the "Rapture" if you like, but it's not what people who hold to this theory are thinking of when they use the word.

If the Millennium immediately follows the Tribulation, then both the Postmillennial theory and the Arapturist theory put the Rapture (or "so-called Rapture") at the same time: right between these two events. So in that scenario, Postmillennial and Arapture are pretty much the same thing.

6.7. Second Coming

Many places in the Bible talk about the Second Coming. Some of the most useful to understanding it:

Acts 1:9-11. Now when He had spoken these things, while they watched, He was taken up, and a cloud received Him out of their sight. And while they looked steadfastly toward heaven as He went up, behold, two men stood by them in white apparel, who also said, "Men of Galilee, why do you stand gazing up into heaven? This *same* Jesus, who was taken up from you into heaven, will so come in like manner as you saw Him go into heaven."

Matthew 24:29-30. Immediately after the tribulation of those days the sun will be darkened, and the moon will not give its light; the stars will fall from heaven, and the powers of the heavens will be shaken. Then the sign of the Son of Man will appear in heaven, and then all the tribes of the earth will mourn, and they will see the Son of Man coming on the clouds of heaven with power and great glory.

Revelation 19:6-7. And I heard, as it were, the voice of a great multitude, as the sound of many waters and as the sound of mighty thunderings, saying, "Alleluia! For the Lord God Omnipotent reigns! Let us be glad and rejoice and give Him glory, for the marriage of the Lamb has come, and His wife has made herself ready."

Revelation 19:11-16. Now I saw heaven opened, and behold, a white horse. And He who sat on him *was* called Faithful and True, and in righteousness He judges and makes war. ... And the armies in heaven, clothed in fine linen, white and clean, followed Him on white horses. Now out of His mouth goes a sharp sword, that with it He should strike the nations. And He Himself will rule them with a rod of iron. He Himself treads the winepress of the fierceness and wrath of Almighty God. And He has on *His* robe and on His thigh a name written: KING OF KINGS AND LORD OF LORDS.

Daniel 7:13-14. "I was watching in the night visions, And behold, *One* like the Son of Man, Coming with the clouds of heaven! He came to the Ancient of Days, And they brought Him near before Him. Then to Him was given dominion and glory and a kingdom, That all peoples, nations, and languages should serve Him. His dominion *is* an everlasting dominion, Which shall not pass away, And His kingdom *the one* Which shall not be destroyed.

There are two very different theories about the Second Coming.

Theory 1: Futurists say that the Second Coming is a future event, when Christ will return in power and glory to establish his Millennial kingdom on Earth. Jesus Christ came the first time as a baby in a manger. He came as a meek human being and allowed himself to be tortured and killed. But when he comes the second time, it will be in power and glory, to destroy his enemies and establish himself as ruler of the world. He's coming back, and this time, he won't be the one getting nailed to a tree! His return will be literal, physical, very visible and very obvious. No one will debate whether or not he has returned.

Theory 2: Full Preterists have a very different view of the Second Coming. They say that Jesus returned in AD 70 to judge the nation of Israel. His return was neither visible nor obvious, and he did not establish a divine kingdom on Earth at that time. He came in judgement, much as God has come in judgment many times throughout history, such as when he rained fire on Sodom and Gomorrah, or when he sent the Babylonians to take Israel captive.

While Full Preterists use the phrase "Second Coming", the term is not really applicable in their system. To Preterists, Christ has "come" many times in many different ways.

Note that the phrase "second coming" does not appear in the Bible. Nowhere does the Bible say that Christ will come to Earth exactly twice. Many Christians, Preterists and Futurists alike, believe that Jesus came to Earth a number of times before he came as a baby in the manger. These are called "pre-incarnation appearances of Christ", or "theophanies", or "Christophanies". For example in Judges 13, we are told that "the Angel of the Lord" appears to Samson's parents, but then his father refers to this "angel" as God. Whether these appearances are God the Father or God the Son or someone or something else is outside the scope of this book. The point here is simply that the idea that Christ might come to Earth more than twice is not a theory peculiar to Preterists.

Partial Preterists combine the views of Futurists and Full Preterists on this point. They say that some verses about Jesus's return are talking about him coming in AD 70 to judge Israel, and that other verses that talk about his return are about a future time when he will come in a visible way to establish a kingdom.

The Futurist view is likely familiar to most Christians. Preterists say that we are misunderstanding what Jesus meant when he talked of his coming here. He didn't mean that he would come in power and glory to judge the world and end history as we know it. Rather, they say, Jesus meant that he was working to judge the Jewish nation for apostasy and for rejecting him, and to protect the Jews who had accepted him – Christian Jews, i.e. Messianic Jews – from the consequences of the destruction of Israel by the Romans. They say that he was working in the same way that God has often worked throughout history: by using people to carry out his will. Like he used Israel to judge the Canaanites and the Moabites, and like he used the Assyrians and the Babylonians to judge Israel.

Evangelicals often assume that the language, "they will see the Son of Man coming on the clouds of heaven with power and great glory" is literal. But not necessarily. Consider this prophecy from Jeremiah.

> Jeremiah 4:13. Behold, he shall come up like clouds, And his chariots like a whirlwind. His horses are swifter than eagles. Woe to us, for we are plundered!

If you read the entire context, it is clearly talking about the conquest of Judah by the Babylonians, which was fulfilled in 587 BC.

Or this prophecy:

> Isaiah 19:1. The burden against Egypt. Behold, the Lord rides on a swift cloud, And will come into Egypt; The idols of Egypt will totter at His presence, And the heart of Egypt will melt in its midst.

Isaiah plainly says that he is talking about a judgement against Egypt. According to the Jewish historian Josephus, this prophecy was fulfilled in 170 BC. (See Josephus's *Antiquities of the Jews*, book 13, chapter 3, section 1.)

We won't go into the details of either prophecy here – they're not about the Second Coming. And that's the point. Both prophecies use words very similar to Jesus's words in Matthew. Matthew: "coming on the clouds of heaven"; Jeremiah: "come up like clouds"; Isaiah: "rides on a swift cloud". Yet Isaiah and Jeremiah are talking about events that were fulfilled in the past, and there is no mention in the Bible or in secular history of God literally and physically appearing in the sky and coming down from Heaven surrounded by clouds. Indeed Jeremiah probably isn't talking about God coming in the clouds at all, but about the king of Babylon doing so. So apparently these words are not meant literally, but symbolically. When discussing Isaiah and Jeremiah, many Bible commentators say that the phrase means that God will act swiftly, like a cloud can travel quickly across the sky. Or that the writer is using thunderclouds and lightning as a symbol of God's power.

Thus, the Preterist says that when it talks about Jesus coming back using similar words, it doesn't mean that he's coming back in a very visible way, literally riding on clouds, to establish his divine kingdom. Rather, it means he is executing divine judgement. He literally came back, but not in a way that was visible to people in general. He came, executed judgement, and returned to Heaven.

On the other hand, recall Acts 1:9-11, quoted at the beginning of this section. This pretty clearly indicates that Jesus left the Earth by floating or flying up into the sky and disappearing into the clouds, and that he will someday return in the same way. Presumably the reverse: he will come down out of the clouds and set foot on the ground. There is no reason to believe that Acts 1 is not talking about literally rising up into clouds. It is not a prophetic symbol.

Both could be true: Jesus could have returned "behind the scenes" in the past to execute judgement, and then he could return again sometime in the future, obviously and visibly, to establish his rule on Earth.

A curious problem is that, by the plain reading, the Apostle Paul expected Christ to return in his lifetime.

1 Thessalonians 4:15-17. According to the Lord's word, we tell you that we who are still alive, who are left until the coming of the Lord, will certainly not precede those who have fallen asleep. For the Lord himself will come down from heaven, with a loud command, with the voice of the archangel and with the trumpet call of God, and the dead in Christ will rise first. After that, we

who are still alive and are left will be caught up together with them in the clouds to meet the Lord in the air. And so we will be with the Lord forever.

Note that when he speaks of Christ's return, he says "*we* who are alive".

If by "the Lord ... will come down from heaven" he means a visible, obvious return, there's clearly a problem here. No such thing happened during Paul's lifetime. Paul was executed by the Romans, probably in AD 67. (Some historians put Paul's death earlier, as early as AD 62. I haven't seen any who put it later.) He was not caught up to meet Christ in the air: his head was cut off by a Roman executioner.

I've heard many Bible teachers explain this by saying that Paul *hoped* that Christ would return during his lifetime, but this didn't happen. I have a problem with that explanation. There's nothing in the text to indicate that this was his private hope and that his statements about this are not inspired by the Holy Spirit. If we just say, "Oh well, Paul was wrong about that", surely that calls all scripture into question. If Paul was wrong in thinking Christ would return in his lifetime, what else was he wrong about? What else in the books written by Paul was his personal hope or private whim, and not inspired scripture? What other parts of the Bible are mistakes made by the writers and not divine inspiration? No. Before I abandon faith in the infallibility of scripture, I'm going to look for other explanations.

Those who say that the First Resurrection is not physical (see section 6.9) say that Paul means that he will see the judgement on Israel that occurred in AD 70. The Jewish War that climaxed with the destruction of Jerusalem in AD 70 began in AD 66. Paul didn't live to see the destruction of Jerusalem, but he did live to see the beginning of the war. If the whole war was God's judgement on Israel, then Paul saw it start. Perhaps it is significant that Paul died just as the war was starting. God told him that he would live to see this judgement, and he lived just long enough to see it and then died.

It is possible the Paul is referring neither to a future

Second Coming nor to the AD 70 judgement of Israel. But if so, I have never heard a theory about just what he is describing. It could not be Christians literally flying up into the air, as this didn't happen in Paul's lifetime. But what? Paul is contrasting what will happen to those still alive with those who have already died. Maybe he's just saying that when resurrection day comes, those who were alive when Christ was on Earth will not have any special precedence over those who died earlier, that the Old Testament dead will rise first and then the New Testament dead will follow, and that modern readers are making too much of "caught up to meet him in the air".

Granted, the problem all comes from one word: "we". But we can't write this off as a problem of translation. The word "we" clearly occurs in the original Greek. In fact in the Greek it's emphatic, like putting it in all capitals in English. We can't just brush off the "we" as Paul casually using an imprecise pronoun.

Some commentators say that Paul's use of "we" is not meant to be literal. The best evidence for this is that elsewhere Paul also includes himself among those who will be resurrected:

1 Corinthians 6:14. And God both raised up the Lord and will also raise us up by His power.

Note that in 1 Thessalonians he said "we" for those who will be caught up to Heaven without dying, while in 1 Corinthians says "us" for those who will be resurrected. Again, the word "us" is clearly present in the Greek.

Thus, it's possible the Paul is using an "editorial 'we'". Like a school teacher might say, "We must all remember to get our homework done tonight". The teacher isn't really among those who have to do the homework, but she says "we" to soften the command. Or like a newspaper commentary or blog post might say, "We are a great nation: We have put a man on the Moon. We have created the Internet." Did the writer have anything to do with putting a man on the Moon or inventing the Internet? Probably not, but he's identifying himself in spirit with the people who did. (Perhaps arrogantly, perhaps in a legitimate sense of community, depending on the context.)

6.8. End of the Age

> Matthew 24:3. Now as He sat on the Mount of Olives, the
> disciples came to Him privately, saying, "Tell us, when will these
> things be? And what *will be* the sign of Your coming, and of the
> end of the age?"

The disciples linked the Second Coming to "the end of the age". What is "the end of the age"?

Christians often understand it to mean "the end of the world". It certainly doesn't mean the end of humanity. The saved will live forever with Christ and the unsaved will live forever in Hades, so there never will be an "end of humanity". It can't mean the end of the world in that sense.

All of history from the Fall of Adam and Eve to the Second Coming is a detour from God's original plan. We were created to live in perfect fellowship with him, but people sinned and separated themselves from God. Christ came to restore a right relationship with God, a process which will not be complete until the Second Coming or the Millennium, or some other future date, depending on which theory proves to be correct. But at some point God will get everything back on track. That is not "the end of the world". It is more like the beginning, after a false start. If you set out to write a novel, and when you typed the first sentence you realized that you had made a typing error, so you deleted it and prepared to start over, would you say that once you had erased the mistake, that the novel was finished? Of course not. It has just started.

So the end of the age is not the end of the world, but rather the end of a particular era in the history of the world. So just what era is that?

We are told several things about the end of the age:

> Matthew 13:39b-42. … the harvest is the end of the age, and the
> reapers are the angels. Therefore as the tares are gathered and
> burned in the fire, so it will be at the end of this age. The Son of

Man will send out His angels, and they will gather out of His kingdom all things that offend, and those who practice lawlessness, and will cast them into the furnace of fire. There will be wailing and gnashing of teeth.

At the end of the age is the judgement, when God separates the saved from the unsaved and condemns the unsaved to Hades.

Matthew 24:3, quoted at the beginning of this section, indicates that the disciples believed that the end of the age would come when Christ returned. In his reply to their question, he never says that this is wrong, so it's fair to conclude that their assumption is correct.

But then here's the funny part.

Hebrews 9:25-26. [N]ot that He should offer Himself often, as the high priest enters the Most Holy Place every year with blood of another— He then would have had to suffer often since the foundation of the world; but now, once at the end of the ages, He has appeared to put away sin by the sacrifice of Himself

In context, Paul is saying that while under the old system the high priest had to offer an animal sacrifice every year, Christ sacrificed himself, and he sacrificed himself once for all time. Christ does not have to come year after year and be crucified over and over again. But note *when* Paul says Christ was crucified: "now ... at the end of the ages".

So the "end of the age" is linked with three events: Judgment Day, the Second Coming, and the Crucifixion.

This is probably evidence in favor of Preterism. The Crucifixion was about AD 34, give or take no more than a couple of years. The Preterist places the Matthew 24 coming of Christ at AD 70. So the Preterist says that the end of the age is, essentially, the end of "Old Testament times", as it gives way to "New Testament times". That is, Christ made the old system of animal sacrifices and ritual law unnecessary. He created a new covenant, a new way for people to relate to God. And so he ended one age and began another. The old age ended with the events wrapped

- 97 -

around his Crucifixion and the destruction of the temple in Jerusalem. Some Preterists say that the judgement Jesus talked about in Matthew 13 must therefore be God's judgement on the nation of Israel in AD 70, when he used the Romans to destroy those who did not accept him while saving those who did. This fits in with all these events being the "end of the age".

Futurists understand Jesus's return as described in Matthew 24 as his Second Coming in power, and the judgement in Matthew 13 as the final judgement of the saved and the unsaved. By this theory, the end of the age is when Christ returns, judges all humanity, and establishes his Millennial kingdom. But then how do you fit in the Crucifixion also being part of the end of the age? The Crucifixion and the Second Coming are separated by at least 2000 years.

Perhaps the end of the age is not a point in time, but a long period stretching from AD 34 to some future time when Christ returns. Personally I find this unlikely. "End of the age" would seem to indicate a point in time, not an era. Saying the end of the age stretched out over 30 or 40 years makes it rather long, but okay, I could buy that. Saying it has lasted 2000 years and is still going on strains plausibility. The "age of the Law" lasted from Moses, circa 1440 BC, to Jesus, circa AD 34, or 1473 years. It seems odd to say that the "age" itself lasted 1473 years but the "end of the age" will last 2000 years or more. If that had been Jesus's and Paul's intent, it seems more likely they would have called this period a new age, not the end of the age.

Perhaps there are two "ends of the ages" here: the end of the Mosaic age in AD 34 to AD 70, and then there's another age, the Church age, that ends with the Second Coming.

By the way, at the start of this section I said that the end of the age is not the end of humanity. It is probably not the end of the world, either. We are told in Revelation 21:1 that the Earth will be destroyed at some point: "Now I saw a new heaven and a new earth, for the first heaven and the first earth had passed away." A time will come when the physical world, this planet, will end. But this is not explicitly linked to the end of the age. Most theories of prophecy do not put the end of the age and the end of the world at the same time.

As we've noted, Preterists put the end of the age at Christ's crucifixion. Obviously the planet Earth was not destroyed at that time.

Pre-Milleniallists say the Second Coming is followed by the Millennium, a period of 1000 years, and after that the Earth is destroyed. So there's at least 1000 years between the two events.

Postmillenniallists put the Second Coming after the Millennium. I think most Post-Mills would put the destruction of the Earth pretty shortly after the Second Coming, so by that theory, the end of the age and the end of the world would be close enough together that they could arguably be said to happen at the same time.

6.9.   Resurrections

> Revelation 20:4b-6. Then *I saw* the souls of those who had been beheaded for their witness to Jesus and for the word of God, who had not worshiped the beast or his image, and had not received *his* mark on their foreheads or on their hands. And they lived and reigned with Christ for a thousand years. But the rest of the dead did not live again until the thousand years were finished. This *is* the first resurrection. Blessed and holy *is* he who has part in the first resurrection. Over such the second death has no power, but they shall be priests of God and of Christ, and shall reign with Him a thousand years.

Christians often speak of "the resurrection" or "resurrection day". But these verses plainly tell us that there will be not one, but two resurrections. There are probably exactly two. Calling one the "first resurrection" implies that there are none before it. If there were any resurrections before this, it wouldn't be the "first". From the fact that it says that "the rest of the dead" are raised in the second resurrection, it seems logical that there can't be any more resurrections after the second, as there is no one left to be raised.

What will we be like after the resurrection? There are two common misconceptions about this.

One is that after the resurrection we become angels. But nowhere does scripture say that we become angels after death. Humans and angels are distinct beings.

There are a few references to saints coming back to speak to people, like when Moses and Elijah came to speak with Jesus and some of the disciples on the Mount of Transfiguration (Matthew 17) or when Samuel appeared to Saul (1 Samuel 28). Nowhere are the people who make such an appearance called angels. We are not told that "the angel of Samuel" spoke to Saul but "the spirit of Samuel".

The Sadducees once asked Jesus about marriage in Eternity. I don't want to get into the details of his answer here, but one point that he made is relevant:

> Matthew 22:30. For in the resurrection they neither marry nor are given in marriage, but are like angels of God in heaven.

Note Jesus said that after the resurrection, we will be "like angels". If we would become actual angels, he would have said, "you will be angels", not "you will be *like* angels". And he didn't say that people will be like angels in general, but only in this one specific way: that they won't marry. That doesn't mean that we won't be like angels in any other way, but it implies that we won't be like angels in all ways.

What sort of bodies will we have? Christians often think of the resurrection body as being "spiritual", something misty and ghost like.

The Bible actually says the opposite:

> 2 Corinthians 5:1-5. For we know that if our earthly house, *this* tent, is destroyed, we have a building from God, a house not made with hands, eternal in the heavens. For in this we groan, earnestly desiring to be clothed with our habitation which is from heaven, if indeed, having been clothed, we shall not be found naked. For we who are in *this* tent groan, being burdened, not because we want to

be unclothed, but further clothed, that mortality may be swallowed up by life

Paul here compares our present bodies to clothes. He says that in eternity we will not be naked, but have better clothes. That is, we will not be souls without a body, but rather will have a better body. He also compares our present body to a tent and our resurrection body to a building. The resurrection body will not be flimsy and insubstantial compared to our present bodies. Just the opposite: it will be more substantial. After all, our present bodies are temporary: they are meant to last maybe 90 years. Somewhere around our 50s our bodies start to wear out and break down. (I speak here from personal experience!) But the resurrection body is meant to last for eternity.

> 1 Corinthians 15:35-39,42b-44. But someone will say, "How are the dead raised up? And with what body do they come?" Foolish one, what you sow is not made alive unless it dies. And what you sow, you do not sow that body that shall be, but mere grain—perhaps wheat or some other *grain.* [38] But God gives it a body as He pleases, and to each seed its own body. ... *The body* is sown in corruption, it is raised in incorruption. It is sown in dishonor, it is raised in glory. It is sown in weakness, it is raised in power. It is sown a natural body, it is raised a spiritual body. There is a natural body, and there is a spiritual body.

I don't claim to fully understand what Paul is saying here. The earthly body is like a seed and the eternal body is like a plant. The seed turns into the plant. So somehow the earthly body turns into the eternal body? I have no idea how this works. Presumably it can't be dependent on there being any recognizable remains of the earthly body. I'm sure Paul was well aware that bodies rot away. Ultimately there is nothing left but at most a skeleton, and at the least, nothing distinguishable at all.

We should concede, or perhaps I should say "clarify", that scripture records a number of times when specific people were raised from the dead. There's no need to go to great lengths here as the details of each incident are not important to the current point, but just to quickly list them:

1. The son of the widow of Zarephath, by Elijah (1 Kings 17:17-24)
2. The son of a Shunammite couple, by Elisha (2 Kings 4:18-37)
3. The man dumped in Elisha's tomb (2 Kings 13:21) A story I find very curious: no one prayed for his resurrection, it was not given as a sign of anything. Why God raised this man is not at all clear.
4. The daughter of Jairus, by Jesus (Mark 5:22-23,35-43)
5. The son of the widow of Nain, by Jesus (Luke 7:11-15)
6. Lazarus, by Jesus (John 11:41-44) You knew this one was in there.
7. Jesus, by God the Father (John 20)
8. A number of saints raised when Jesus died (Matthew 27:52-53)
9. Tabitha, by Peter (Acts 9:36-42)
10. Eutychus, by Paul (Acts 20:9-11) The first man recorded to fall asleep during a sermon, fell out a window and was killed.

In a couple of these stories, it may be that the person was not actually dead, but in a coma or some such. But others clearly say the person was dead.

It's possible that there have been other similar revivals in history that didn't get recorded in the Bible. I'd think such a revival would be a big enough deal that it would have been mentioned, but who knows? Hebrews 11:35 mentions unnamed resurrections, perhaps in addition to the ones listed here.

We may call these "resurrections", but they are fundamentally different from the two "real" resurrections. Other than Jesus, these people were raised in their Earthly, mortal bodies. They were not given glorified new bodies like we are told will happen when we are resurrected. Presumably they all died again later: I don't think Lazarus and Tabitha and so on are still alive. These were not resurrections in the same sense. They were temporary revivals. So there's no conflict between saying "only two resurrections" and recognizing these 9 or 10 incidents.

Jesus's resurrection is in a different category from the others. Jesus is called the "first fruits" of the resurrection (1 Corinthians 15:20). Quite simply, Jesus is a special case.

We're given a pretty specific timeline for the two resurrections. The first happens just before the Millennium begins. The second happens after the Millennium.

Futurists and Partial Preterists say that these are two literal, physical resurrections. Some of the dead are physically raised in the first; the rest of the dead are physically raised in the second.

Full Preterists say that the first resurrection is spiritual, and only the second resurrection is physical. In the first resurrections, souls are restored from spiritual death. In the second resurrection, bodies are restored from physical death.

Revelation says the first resurrection comes before the Millennium. By most Full Preterist timelines, we are in the Millennium now. So the first resurrection has already happened. Clearly we do not see the resurrected righteous dead walking around the world now. So to make the Full Preterist view work, you have to say one of three things:

One, you could come up with an alternate timeline, say the Millennium hasn't started yet.

Two, the righteous dead were resurrected and are now in Heaven, and when the Bible talks of them reigning with Christ, it means that they are reigning from Heaven. You have to further assume that their resurrected bodies have no connection to their physical bodies: the physical bodies remain in the grave, unchanged, while their resurrected bodies are in Heaven. This would seem to contradict 1 Corinthians 15, but that's a difficult passage so maybe not.

Or three, the first resurrection is not literal and physical, but something else.

Most Full Preterists choose option three.

So they'll say that when Christ died and rose again, there was a "spiritual resurrection". People were freed from the bondage of sin and the law and given new life.

There are problems with this theory. The plain reading of Revelation 20 is that these are two physical resurrections. It says that those raised in the first resurrection were people who were beheaded for their faith. They were physically dead, not just "spiritually dead". And I think it really strains the text to interpret the two resurrections as being fundamentally different in kind, one spiritual and one physical. Also, we're told that in the second resurrection, "the rest" of the dead are raised. But if the first resurrection is spiritual rather than physical, wouldn't those resurrected the first time need to be resurrected again the second time?

This is one of those cases where I think to myself, If you were coming to the text with no preconceptions, with no theory in your mind in advance, what would you understand it to say? I am always suspicious of interpretations that say, "Yes, it *sounds* like it means X, but really it means Y, and I know it means Y because that's the only way I can make it fit into my bigger theory." I don't rule out such explanations. Maybe what seems like the "plain reading" is our own false assumptions. But we should consider such interpretations cautiously.

Frankly, if I was a Full Preterist, I think I'd be pursuing my option "two" above, or maybe possibly option "one".

Some commentators say that there are separate resurrections of the saved and the unsaved. For example, they point to:

> Luke 14:14. And you will be blessed … for you shall be repaid at the resurrection of the just."

If there's a "resurrection of the just", then there must be a separate resurrection for the unjust.

John 5:28b-29. For the hour is coming in which all who are in the graves will hear His voice and come forth—those who have done good, to the resurrection of life, and those who have done evil, to the resurrection of condemnation.

They read this to say that there are two resurrections: one of the good and one of the evil.

Some Futurists say that the saved are resurrected along with the Rapture, just before the start of the Tribulation. (Or halfway through the Tribulation, for Mid-Tribbers.) They use 1 Thessalonians 4:15 as their main text for this. Then they say that the unsaved are not raised until later:

Revelation 20:12-15. And I saw the dead, small and great, standing before God, and books were opened. And another book was opened, which is *the Book* of Life. And the dead were judged according to their works, by the things which were written in the books. The sea gave up the dead who were in it, and Death and Hades delivered up the dead who were in them. And they were judged, each one according to his works. Then Death and Hades were cast into the lake of fire. This is the second death. And anyone not found written in the Book of Life was cast into the lake of fire.

So Revelation 20:12 is the separate resurrection of the unsaved that John mentions, at which they are judged and sentenced to Hell.

Personally, I find this unconvincing. Yes, there are two different groups. Sometimes scriptures discussing the resurrection mention both groups, sometimes just one, and sometimes just the other. Just because the Bible distinguishes the saved from the unsaved when discussing the resurrection doesn't mean that these things happen at different times. Like if I said, "In the election, some people will vote for the Republican and some for the Democrat", I don't think that would justify you in concluding that the vote must occur on two different days. Indeed John 5 sounds to me like it's saying that everyone is raised at the same time, and then judged one way or the other, not that there are separate resurrections for the two groups.

Some who adhere to this theory connect the "first resurrection" of Revelation 20 to the resurrection of the saved and the "second resurrection" to the resurrection of the unsaved. I don't think this works. The plain reading of Revelation 20 is that the first resurrection is not all the saved, but only those who were martyred for refusing to worship the Beast. We could debate here just what the "Beast" is (see section 6.19), whether it is something that is specific to one time and place or represents some enemy of Christianity throughout history. But even if we interpret this very broadly, and say that when he talks of those persecuted by the Beast he means Christians persecuted at any time in history, still, he specifically says those who were "beheaded" for their faith. Surely you don't have to be beheaded, or even martyred by any means, to be saved. I just don't see how you can read the first resurrection here as being all the saved. And if the second resurrection is "the rest of the dead", then it must include many saved people.

In my opinion, the Bible pretty clearly spells out that there will be exactly two resurrections. Therefore, any other mention of resurrections must be tied to these two. Any theory that calls for three or four or ten resurrections is ignoring Revelation 20. I can accept that there might be a special case here and there. Like Jesus is clearly held out as a special case. But that's the only special case I see.

Some try to drag the first resurrection out into a long period of time. They say it began with the righteous dead raised at Christ's crucifixion, continued through Christ's resurrection, and then up to the Rapture and maybe later.

That only fits Revelation 20 if you take a Postmillennial view. Revelation 20 says that Satan is bound to begin the Millennium, then there's the first resurrection, then there's the Millennium, and then there's the second resurrection. So for the first resurrection to begin while Christ was on Earth, Satan had to be bound about the time of the crucifixion. We also have to assume that the Millennium is not a literal 1000 years. I don't see any way to fit an "extended first resurrection" in to a Pre-Trib /

Pre-Mill scenario.

6.10. Book of Life

There's not much controversy on this, but we need to discuss it to set the stage for discussion of judgment.

The Book of Life is mentioned once in Philippians and seven times in Revelation.

The key passage is:

Revelation 20:12, 15. And I saw the dead, small and great, standing before God, and books were opened. And another book was opened, which is *the Book* of Life. And the dead were judged according to their works, by the things which were written in the books. ... And anyone not found written in the Book of Life was cast into the lake of fire.

Likewise, Revelation 21:27 tells us that only those whose names are in the Book of Life will be admitted to New Jerusalem, the Paradise that God has created for the saved.

So the Book of Life is a list of those who are saved, those who are not condemned to Hell. Presumably it is those who meet God's criteria for salvation, namely:

Romans 10:9. [I]f you confess with your mouth the Lord Jesus and believe in your heart that God has raised Him from the dead, you will be saved.

And:

Ephesians 2:8-9. For by grace you have been saved through faith, and that not of yourselves; *it is* the gift of God, not of works, lest anyone should boast

It is, perhaps, interesting that almost all we know about the Book of Life comes from Revelation. Besides that there is just one brief reference in Philippians:

Philippians 4:3. And I urge you also, true companion, help these women who labored with me in the gospel, with Clement also, and the rest of my fellow workers, whose names *are* in the Book of Life.

And that's it, that's all Philippians says about it.

Revelation was written by John, while Philippians was written by Paul. John presumably learned about the Book of Life when God showed him the visions that make up most of the book of Revelation. But how did Paul learn about it? He couldn't have learned about it from John, because Revelation was written when John was in prison on the Island of Patmos, which was around AD 96, while Philippians was written about AD 62, over 30 years earlier. (Some commentators, especially Preterists, put the writing of Revelation in the late 60s. But I've never seen a dating scheme that puts Philippians after Revelation.) It would seem that God must have given some separate revelation to Paul. But then Paul tells us almost nothing.

Note an interesting thing here. Revelation 20:12 says that the dead will be judged by their works. But then just a few verses later, Revelation 20:15 says that they will be judged based on whether their names are in the Book of Life. So are people saved by works? Or by having their names in the Book of Life?

You might say that I was wrong when I said that the Book of Life lists those who have faith in Christ, and say instead that it is a list of those who did sufficient good works. But this creates several problems. First and most important, the Bible clearly says on many occasions that salvation is *not* by works. Second, if the intent of Revelation 20 was that salvation was by works, then the books with the record of what everyone did in life would be all that was needed to judge. What, then, is the Book of Life and why is it needed?

I believe the resolution is this: Based on our works, we all deserve Hell. So when God judges the dead by their works, he is saying, see, look at all these sins you have committed. You deserve to go to Hell. Then he checks if the person has accepted Christ and thus is freed from the punishment for his sin. If not, the person is condemned to Hell. (I say "he checks" metaphorically here. Presumably God doesn't forget and need to look it up on the computer.)

It is very much like a human judge reviewing a prisoner's sentence. He goes over the record and says something like, "I see you have been convicted of second degree murder. The penalty for that is 15 years in prison" You know you are guilty and you know you deserve the sentence. But then he checks your petition to the governor for amnesty. If the governor has said no, the sentence is carried out. But if the governor has granted amnesty, then you are free. So you are judged by your works, but in the end, you can escape the penalty for your crimes by the mercy or grace of the governor.

The criminal who is not given amnesty cannot say that his sentence was unjust. He committed the crime. He got exactly what he deserved.

In our case, we have all committed sins deserving of Hell. God recounts our sins so that no one can claim that the penalty is unjust. You cannot escape the penalty by proving that you are innocent, because you are not innocent. The only escape is to appeal for amnesty, that is, for the grace of God through Jesus Christ.

6.11. Bema Seat Judgment

"Bema" is a Greek word meaning a platform or dais. It was routinely used to refer to the platform on which a judge's chair was placed. Thus, a "bema seat" was a place where a judge sat.

There are two places where the Bible discusses the "bema seat" of Christ. In both cases "bema" is translated "judgement seat" in the New King James Version quoted here, as well as in most other English translations. That is, you probably won't see the word "bema" in your English Bible. But when Christians want to distinguish these two passages from other verses that talk about judgement, they sometimes refer to these as the "bema seat judgement".

2 Corinthians 5:10. For we must all appear before the judgment seat of Christ, that each one may receive the things *done* in the body, according to what he has done, whether good or bad.

Romans 14:10-12. But why do you judge your brother? Or why do you show contempt for your brother? For we shall all stand before the judgment seat of Christ. For it is written: *"As* I live, says the LORD, Every knee shall bow to Me, And every tongue shall confess to God."* So then each of us shall give account of himself to God.

Some Christians point out that the term "bema seat" was used for judges at a sporting match, for the place where prizes were handed out to the winners. Think of Olympic contestants being handed gold, silver, and bronze medals.

They theorize that this is the sort of judgement intended in these verses. At the bema seat, Christ will judge the saved. This isn't where he condemns some to Hell and admits others to Paradise. Rather, this is the place where he gives rewards to those who have performed exceptional service. Like at the Olympics, the most accomplished athletes are given gold medals. The losers aren't beaten and imprisoned; they just get nothing.

We could relate this to:

1 Corinthians 3:13. Each one's work will become clear; for the Day will declare it, because it will be revealed by fire; and the fire will test each one's work, of what sort it is. If anyone's work which he has built on *it* endures, he will receive a reward. If anyone's work is burned, he will suffer loss; but he himself will be saved, yet so as through fire.

Our salvation is not dependent on doing good works. We are saved by grace, not by works. But Christ will reward good works. Perhaps the implication is that he will punish bad works, or this may mean that lack of good works results in loss of a potential reward as opposed to actual punishment.

On the other hand, the word "bema" was also used for the place where a judge sat to preside over criminal trials and hand out punishments to those found guilty. In fact, nowhere does the

Bible use "bema" to refer to judging at a sporting match, but it does use the word several times to refer to criminal trials.

For example, when Jesus was put on trial before Pontius Pilate, Matthew 27:19 says that Pilate sat on "the judgement seat" – "bema" in Greek. When the Jews had Paul arrested and put on trial before Gallio, Acts 18:16 refers to Gallio sitting on "the judgement seat" – again, "bema".

Romans 14 specifically talks about "judging your brother" before mentioning the bema seat, so it's plausible to say that this is talking about a judgment specifically of believers. But then in context, it could mean that *all* people will be judged, and that "all" here includes believers. You could read it either way.

Read the context of 2 Corinthians and it's equally subject to both interpretations.

Clearly, from 1 Corinthians 3 we see that a believer's works will be judged and rewards given. So one might say that whether this is what the bema seat judgment is about, or whether that happens at some other place and time, is not particularly important. But it is important if we are trying to fit together all the pieces of Bible prophecy.

6.12. Great White Throne Judgment

A pretty fundamental teaching of Christianity is that a day will come when God will judge all people.

There are a number of references in the Bible to a time of judgment. Christians disagree whether all of these are talking about the same event, one great judgment of all people, or whether there are several different judgments.

Some identify three separate judgments:

The Sheep and Goats Judgment:

Matthew 25:31-34, 41, 46. When the Son of Man comes in His glory, and all the holy angels with Him, then He will sit on the throne of His glory. All the nations will be gathered before Him, and He will separate them one from another, as a shepherd divides his sheep from the goats. And He will set the sheep on His right hand, but the goats on the left. Then the King will say to those on His right hand, 'Come, you blessed of My Father, inherit the kingdom prepared for you from the foundation of the world ... Then He will also say to those on the left hand, 'Depart from Me, you cursed, into the everlasting fire prepared for the devil and his angels. ... And these will go away into everlasting punishment, but the righteous into eternal life."

The Bema Seat Judgment, as we discussed in the previous section:

2 Corinthians 5:10. For we must all appear before the judgment seat of Christ, that each one may receive the things *done* in the body, according to what he has done, whether good or bad.

And the Great White Throne Judgment:

Revelation 20:10-15. The devil, who deceived them, was cast into the lake of fire and brimstone where the beast and the false prophet *are*. And they will be tormented day and night forever and ever. Then I saw a great white throne and Him who sat on it, from whose face the earth and the heaven fled away. And there was found no place for them. And I saw the dead, small and great, standing before God, and books were opened. And another book was opened, which is *the Book* of Life. And the dead were judged according to their works, by the things which were written in the books. The sea gave up the dead who were in it, and Death and Hades delivered up the dead who were in them. And they were judged, each one according to his works. Then Death and Hades were cast into the lake of fire. This is the second death. And anyone not found written in the Book of Life was cast into the lake of fire.

The "three judgments" theory assumes the Premillennial theory, that is, it assumes that the Second Coming of Christ comes before the Millennium, and that the Millennium is a time when Christ rules directly and physically on Earth.

By this theory, the Sheep and Goats Judgment occurs at the time of Christ's return, and therefore before the Millennium. It is when Christ decides who will be permitted into his Millennial Kingdom.

At the Great White Throne Judgment, Christ judges unbelievers. These are condemned to Hell because of their unbelief, with the degree of punishment determined by their deeds in this life. The Great White Throne Judgment is clearly put after the Millennium.

At the Bema Seat Judgment, Christ judges believers, and gives rewards to those who have done particularly good works. Note this is not a doctrine of works: the theory is not that you are saved because you did good works. Rather, you are saved by faith in Christ, but you may get rewards based on your good works. If the Bema Seat Judgment is a separate event, we are not given any serious clues about when it happens, so it could be fit into a timeline in many places.

Others say that there is only one judgment, and that these three passages are all talking about the same event. By this theory, the Sheep and Goats Judgment is not about deciding who enters the Millennium, but about who is admitted to Paradise and who is condemned to Hell. As the Great White Throne Judgment is clearly about determining who is condemned to Hell, then the Great White Throne Judgment and the Sheep and Goats Judgment must be the same event. And if both the saved and the unsaved are being judged at the same time, than the Bema Seat must also be the same event.

There are other places in the Bible that talk about a judgment day besides these three, i.e. the Sheep and Goats, the Great White Throne, and the Bema Seat. Advocates of the "three judgments" theory believe that all other references to a judgment day are to one of these three. And of course advocates of the "one judgment" theory believe that all other references are to the one judgment.

I think the key reasoning that leads people to a "three judgments" theory is this:

Read Revelation 20 carefully, and you may note that while it clearly says that at the Great White Throne Judgment the unsaved are condemned to Hell, there is no mention of what happens to the saved. This leads some to say that this judgment is only a judgment of the unsaved.

But at the Sheep and Goats Judgment people are divided into two groups, the righteous and the unrighteous. So if the Great White Throne is only for the unrighteous, it cannot be the same event as the Sheep and Goats. So there must be two separate judgments.

We are explicitly told that believers *will* be judged at the Bema Seat. And we are told that this is a judgment of their works. But if salvation is by faith and not works, then this cannot be a judgment of whether or not they are saved, but must instead be a judgment for handing out of rewards. So this is not a judgment where the saved are separated from the unsaved, so it cannot be the same as Sheep and Goats.

Thus we are left with three judgments: all people, at Sheep and Goats; just the saved, at the Bema Seat; and just the unsaved, at the Great White Throne.

But God condemns people to Hell at the Great White Throne. So if that's not the same as Sheep and Goats, then Sheep and Goats must not be about who goes to Heaven and who goes to Hell. It must be about something else. The text mentions entering Christ's kingdom. So, they say, maybe this is about, not entering Heaven, but about entering Christ's Millennial kingdom.

The one-judgment person replies that in the Sheep and Goats Judgment, the unsaved are condemned to "the everlasting fire prepared for the devil and his angels" (Matthew 25:41). In the Great White Throne Judgement, the unsaved are condemned to "the lake of fire" (Revelation 20:15), and just a few verses earlier we are told that the devil is also cast into the lake of fire (Revelation 20:10). This sounds awfully similar.

Furthermore, we are told that at the Sheep and Goats Judgment the righteous enter "into eternal life" (Matthew 25:46). The reward for the righteous is not a kingdom that lasts for 1000 years, but a kingdom that lasts for eternity.

So it's more plausible to conclude that the Sheep and Goats Judgment and the Great White Throne Judgment are the same thing.

So why doesn't the description of the Great White Throne Judgment in Revelation 20 mention the saved entering Paradise? But it does: you have to turn the page. Revelation 21 is all about the New Earth and the New Jerusalem, the paradise where the saved will live for eternity. Revelation 20 flows right into Revelation 21.

At that point it seems likely that the Bema Seat is also the same event, but this is difficult to prove.

Perhaps I've made it obvious here that I find the "one judgment" theory more convincing.

6.13. New Heaven & Earth

Revelation 21:1. Now I saw a new heaven and a new earth, for the first heaven and the first earth had passed away. Also there was no more sea.

2 Peter 3:10-13. But the day of the Lord will come as a thief in the night, in which the heavens will pass away with a great noise, and the elements will melt with fervent heat; both the earth and the works that are in it will be burned up. Therefore, since all these things will be dissolved, what manner *of persons* ought you to be in holy conduct and godliness, looking for and hastening the coming of the day of God, because of which the heavens will be dissolved, being on fire, and the elements will melt with fervent heat? Nevertheless we, according to His promise, look for new heavens and a new earth in which righteousness dwells.

Matthew 24:35. [Jesus said] Heaven and earth will pass away, but My words will by no means pass away.

Isaiah 65:17-18. For behold, I create new heavens and a new earth; And the former shall not be remembered or come to mind. But be glad and rejoice forever in what I create; For behold, I create Jerusalem *as* a rejoicing, And her people a joy.

Isaiah 66:22-23. For as the new heavens and the new earth Which I will make shall remain before Me," says the LORD, "So shall your descendants and your name remain. And it shall come to pass *That* from one New Moon to another, And from one Sabbath to another, All flesh shall come to worship before Me," says the LORD.

The obvious question here is, when God speaks of a "new Earth", does he mean literally a new planet, a new physical globe hanging in space? Or is this figurative, like after some great political upheaval or technological change someone might say, "It's a whole new world"?

Let's put aside discussion of a new Heaven for a moment, and deal with the easier, but still difficult, new Earth.

Theory 1: Futurists and Partial Preterists generally say that this is a literal new Earth. After the Second Coming and the Millennium, God will destroy this planet and create a new planet for people to live on. Perhaps because people have done so much damage to God's original perfect creation through pollution and violence, and/or because the world is badly damaged by God's judgments during Noah's Flood or the Tribulation. Either way, the world is no longer the perfect place it was created to be; it is not suitable for a paradise where the saved can spend eternity. So God destroys the world and creates a new one.

Theory 2: Full Preterists say the new Earth is figurative. When Christ came, he radically changed the world. People are no longer under bondage to sin. The old system of animal sacrifices is abolished and we now have grace through Christ. It's a whole new world.

A variation on this is that the Church is radically transforming the world through the power of the Gospel.

Theory 3: This refers to the Millennium. When Christ returns, he overthrows all existing human governments and creates a new world order under his rule. This is more consistent with a Futurist or Partial Preterist view.

The point of the passage in 2 Peter is that we should be worrying more about eternal things than about things in this life, because some day this world will be destroyed. This makes sense if we take it either literally or figuratively. This world is only temporary, so we should not be too fixated on things of this world. That could mean the physical world is only temporary, or it could mean that the things of this world – our jobs and houses and social causes and whatever – are only temporary.

The reference in Revelation 21 to "no more sea" sounds more like he is talking about a new physical planet. It's quite comprehensible to say, "God showed me a new planet that he had created, and this new planet had no oceans." It's a very strange and unclear thing to say if he means a new "world system". If he means that the Church will change the world, what does it mean to say that there is no more ocean? Perhaps the ocean is a symbol for something, but what?

Isaiah 65 and 66 are trickier. In Isaiah 64 the prophet speaks to God about how Israel has been destroyed and laid waste. In 65 and 66 God replies with a promise of a future golden age. He speaks of a time of peace and prosperity. It's not clear – to me, anyway – whether he is speaking of a golden age within the normal course of history, or the Millennium, or eternity. If the new Earth is literal, of course it would have to be a time after the Second Coming and after the Millennium.

What makes me think that he is not speaking of eternity is this:

> Isaiah 65:20. No more shall an infant from there *live but a few* days, Nor an old hman who has not fulfilled his days; For the child shall die one hundred years old, But the sinner *being* one hundred years old shall be accursed.

If he's talking of a golden age in normal human history, a promise that children will not die in infancy but will routinely live to be 100 makes a lot of sense. But if he's speaking of eternity, presumably children won't live to be 100, but will live forever.

- 117 -

It's possible that he's mixing different times together here, that he talks of a new Earth that he will create after the Second Coming, and then talks about a golden age that will come before that time. The point of these chapters is clearly to say that God will give Israel better times in the future. Like someone talking about his dreams might say, "Someday I hope to travel the world, and get a big house and a fancy car, and marry a beautiful girl, and be famous." He presumably doesn't mean that he expects to do all these things at the same time. He doesn't expect to be living in the big house at the same time that he's travelling the world, etc.

The word translated "element" here is the Greek word ΣΤΟΙΧΕΙΑ ("stoicheia"). This means an indivisible unit of something. It was often used to refer to letters of the alphabet: they are the smallest building blocks of language, from which words and sentences are built. Plato used this word to refer to atoms.

Perhaps I should explain at this point that the ancient Greeks had theories about atoms that were in some ways very much like modern atomic theory. Greek philosophers and scientists reasoned: What if you cut something in half? Aristotle used a piece of cheese as an example. You get two smaller pieces of cheese. What if you cut one of these in half again? You get yet smaller pieces of cheese. So, he asked, if you kept cutting this cheese again and again, do you get smaller pieces of cheese forever? Or do you eventually reach a point where you have the smallest possible piece of cheese, and anything smaller than that is not cheese, but things that must be combined to make cheese? We call these things "atoms" or "elements".

If there are such things as atoms, then maybe we can break apart the atoms that make things up and recombine them in different ways. And in fact we find that we can do this: today we call it "chemical reactions".

An example the Greeks noticed was that you could burn a piece of wood, turning it into fire, smoke, and ash. And so they concluded that one kind of atom was fire. Remove fire from wood and the atoms that are left make ash.

At that point the Greeks got it wrong. They concluded that there are four elements: fire, air, water, and earth. Today we know that there are at least 91 naturally occurring elements (a few more may exist in natural but unusual conditions), and 27 more have been created in the laboratory. But before you make fun of the ancient Greeks, ask yourself honestly how far you would have gotten if you hadn't been told the right answers in chemistry class!

My point on this little side trail is that if Peter is talking about the world literally being destroyed, the mention of elements makes sense, and displays some serious technical sophistication. He is saying not just that there will be fires all over the world, or even that the world will be blown up in some huge explosion, but that the very elements, the atoms that make up the planet Earth, will be destroyed.

Advocates of a figurative destruction point out that the word "elements" can also be used for things that make up a society. Other than this debatable verse, there is no place in the Bible that uses "elements" to refer to chemical elements, but several places that use it to refer to elements of society. For example:

> Galatians 4:3. Even so we, when we were children, were in bondage under the elements of the world.

> Colossians 2:20. Therefore, if you died with Christ from the basic principles of the world, why, as *though* living in the world, do you subject yourselves to regulations?

("Principles" in Colossians 3:20 is the same Greek word translated "elements" in 2 Peter 3 and Galatians 4.)

Thus, the Preterist says, "elements" in 2 Peter 3 means the pieces that make up the world system.

But if "the Earth" means "the world system created by sinful humans" and "elements" means "the pieces of that system", presumably corrupt governments and greedy businesses and criminal gangs and so on, why does Peter sound so literal when he talks of their destruction? If he simply said, "the world will be destroyed", one could say that this means "corrupt powers will be overthrown" as well as "the physical planet will be destroyed". But Peter doesn't just say that it will be destroyed, he says it will "melt with fervent heat", there will be "great noise", it will be "burned up" and "dissolved". This is exactly the sort of language we would expect someone to use if we was speaking of something literally being burned up. It is not at all clear what this means if this is all a metaphor for "corrupt powers will be overthrown".

So what does a "new Heaven" mean?
The Bible uses the word "heaven" in at least three ways.

One, the sky, the place where clouds are and where birds fly.

Psalm 104:12. By them the birds of the heavens have their home; They sing among the branches.

Job 35:5. Look to the heavens and see; And behold the clouds— They are higher than you.

Two, outer space, where the stars and planets are.

Genesis 15:5a. Then He brought him outside and said, "Look now toward heaven, and count the stars if you are able to number them."

And three, the place from which God rules and where his throne is.

Deuteronomy 26:15a. Look down from Your holy habitation, from heaven, and bless Your people Israel and the land which You have given us.

This isn't just an interpretation imposed on the Bible. In one place the Bible specifically talks about three Heavens.

2 Corinthians 12:2,4. I know a man in Christ who fourteen years ago—whether in the body I do not know, or whether out of the body I do not know, God knows—such a one was caught up to the third heaven ... how he was caught up into Paradise and heard inexpressible words, which it is not lawful for a man to utter.

Thus Paradise is the "third heaven". It is at least plausible to say that the sky and space are the first and second.

If the new heaven is literal, which heaven is new?

A new sky is not only plausible but inevitable. If the Earth is totally destroyed, the air around it, the birds and the clouds and so forth, will go too.

It's possible that he means that all of space, the whole universe, will be destroyed and a new universe created. My "gut feel" is that this is unlikely. While people have corrupted this Earth, we have barely touched the other planets in our own solar system. Only one human artifact has ever left out solar system – the Voyager 1 space probe. It will take 40,000 years for it to reach another star.

Others point to Genesis, where God cursed the ground because of Adam's sin:

Genesis 3:17. Then to Adam He said, "Because you have heeded the voice of your wife, and have eaten from the tree of which I commanded you, saying, 'You shall not eat of it': Cursed *is* the ground for your sake; In toil you shall eat *of* it All the days of your life.

They say that at this time God cursed the entire universe, that the entire universe is now subject to decay and death. If that's the case, then perhaps God will eventually create a whole new universe to replace the cursed one.

Or, by a "new heaven" the Bible means that the new Earth will be in a different place in space. God won't create the new Earth in the same place that the old Earth presently is, but orbiting some other star. Then when people look up at the night sky they will see different constellations. It will be a "new heaven".

It seems unlikely that God will destroy the place where he has his throne. Whether or not human sin has corrupted other star systems, we surely have not corrupted God's habitation. People have physically despoiled this Earth, but we have not harmed his throne room in any way.

Personally, I find the literal interpretation more plausible. If you interpret these verses literally, they make simple and obvious sense. 2 Peter says that the world will be burned to a cinder. He describes the world being set on fire, and everything melting in the heat. It makes sense if read literally.

You can read it figuratively, but if Peter intended to say that religious institutions or governments would be overthrown, why didn't he just say that? Read the verses leading up to the statement about the world being destroyed by fire:

> 2 Peter 3:5b-8. ... by the word of God the heavens were of old, and the earth standing out of water and in the water, by which the world *that* then existed perished, being flooded with water. But the heavens and the earth *which* are now preserved by the same word, are reserved for fire until the day of judgment and perdition of ungodly men.

Clearly Peter is referring to the original creation and to Noah's Flood. When he talks about water he means literal water. He contrasts the waters that destroyed the world in Noah's day with the fire that will destroy the world at some future date. It seems odd to link the destruction of the literal, physical world in the time of Noah with the destruction of a symbolic "world system" in the future, and to compare literal water with symbolic fire. Nothing in the text indicates a shift from literal to symbolic. Sometimes a speaker will compare a literal flood to a symbolic flood, but it's very odd to compare a literal flood to a symbolic fire. Possible, but odd.

Similarly, in Revelation John says that the new Earth has no oceans. This makes a lot of sense if he's describing a new physical planet. If God showed him the Earth from space – presumably he'd have no trouble recognizing it if God showed him a view from above the Mediterranean Sea, he'd seen maps -- and then God showed him this new planet from space, if the new planet had no oceans that would be a very obvious difference. It might well be the first thing one would notice.

If it's symbolic, what does it mean to say the new Earth has no oceans? If the text simply said, "God will destroy the world and create a new world", I could accept saying that this might mean he will destroy governments and institutions and replace them with new ones. Saying he will burn up the elements is a stretch, but maybe that means that he won't just destroy these institutions as a whole, but he will destroy every part of them. But what does it mean to say that the new world he will create will have no oceans? Perhaps oceans are a symbol for something, but what? Why is there no clue what it represents? In fairness, Revelation is filled with symbols that are not always explained, so maybe.

If the "new Earth" refers to a new world system, then what is a "new Heaven"? It's certainly true that the Earth has become corrupt. It's not unreasonable to say that what we need is not "reform" but the total destruction of present worldly systems to then be replaced by a completely new system. But people haven't corrupted Heaven. Why would Heaven need to be replaced?

In 2 Peter, Peter says that the new Heaven and Earth are in the future. "The day of the Lord will come ...", not "has come". So if it's figurative, it can't be that Christ's death and resurrection destroyed the old world system and created a new world. By the time 2 Peter was written, Christ was already resurrected. The theory that the Church creates a new world is also problematic. We could debate just when Christ created the Church, but it's hard to see how you could put it after his Ascension. He might describe it as a process going on right now: "all these things are being dissolved", etc. But he wouldn't put it in the future. 2 Peter is consistent with the new Earth being a future Millennium. But Peterists say we are in the Millennium now. Preterists are trying to put the new Heaven and new Earth in the past. But you can't do that without ignoring 2 Peter. Maybe, possibly, you could say that Peter means that the process of creating the new Earth began with Christ's crucifixion and resurrection, continues today, and will be complete at some time in the future. But Peter's language uses future tense throughout.

The essence of the Preterist theory is that all these prophecies have been fulfilled. Therefore, the Preterist *has* to say that the new Heaven and new Earth are figurative. Generally Preterists try to fit the new Heaven and new Earth in at about the time of Christ's first coming: either Jesus created a new world through his coming, or the Church has created or is in the process of creating a new world by spreading the Gospel. Obviously the physical world was not literally burned up when Christ came, so the only way to fit these verses into the Preterist theory is to make them symbolic.

6.14. Rosh and Friends

The name "Rosh" is found in Ezekiel's prophecy of a great battle. Many commentators believe this is the same battle that Revelation calls the Battle of Armageddon: we'll get to this battle in section 6.15.

> Ezekiel 38:2-6. "Son of man, set your face against Gog, of the land of Magog, the prince of Rosh, Meshech, and Tubal, and prophesy against him, and say, 'Thus says the Lord GOD: "Behold, I *am* against you, O Gog, the prince of Rosh, Meshech, and Tubal. I will turn you around, put hooks into your jaws, and lead you out, with all your army, horses, and horsemen, all splendidly clothed, a great company *with* bucklers and shields, all of them handling swords. Persia, Ethiopia, and Libya are with them, all of them *with* shield and helmet; Gomer and all its troops; the house of Togarmah *from* the far north and all its troops—many people *are* with you.

If you compare this to other English translations, you may be surprised to see that there is no mention of Rosh. The original King James, for example, says "Son of man, set thy face against Gog, the land of Magog, the chief prince of Meshech and Tubal."

(Note: You may also see that other translations say "Meshek" instead of "Meschech". That's just an alternate spelling.)

The Hebrew word ראש ("rosh") is a word meaning "chief". It can also be a proper name. Just like the English word "mark" can mean "a visible impression", as in, "he made a mark with a pencil", and can also be a proper name. So some scholars read these verses as saying that Gog is the "chief prince" of Meshech and Tubal. That is, chief prince of two places. Others say that it means that Gog is the "prince" of Rosh, Meshech, and Tubal. That is, (ordinary) prince of three places. Both readings are grammatically possible from the Hebrew.

Those who see Rosh as a name usually associate it with Russia. There's the obvious similarity in sound – stronger still if you consider that "Russia" comes from the older name "Rus". Russia is "far north" from Israel. Josephus, the ancient Jewish historian, wrote that Magog is the people that the Greeks call Scythians. (*Antiquities of the Jews*, 1:6:1) The Scythians lived in what today is south-western Russia. Advocates of the "Russia theory" sometimes make the further argument that "Meshech" means Moscow.

Those who see "rosh" as meaning "chief" say that the "Russia" evidence is weak. Most ancient writers put Magog in Asia Minor, that is, modern Turkey. Hippolytus of Rome, a Christian; Pliny the Elder, a pagan; and Maimonides, a Jew; all put Magog in Asia Minor. The Greek historian Herodotus said that the Scythians originated in Asia Minor and migrated to what we today call Russia, which may explain Josephus. Meshech and Tubal are all also traditionally placed in Turkey. As Ezekiel lumps Magog in with these others, it makes sense if they are all in the same region. The reference to "far north" could apply to Turkey: it is also directly north of Israel. (Is it "far" north? How far is far?) This was pretty much the universal interpretation until the 1700s.

The connection of Meshech with Moscow appears to be based solely on the similarity in the names. I am unable to find any historical or geographical argument linking the two. This is very weak. "Meshech" sounds like "Michigan", too, but I sincerely doubt that Ezekiel's prophecy was about Michigan. (Not that this isn't a very evil place!)

On the other hand, the word "Russia" did not exist in Ezekiel's day. Russia would not exist until the late 800s AD. So if God wanted to tell Ezekiel about the future Russian nation, there was no name for it. Perhaps God arranged for the Hebrew word for "chief" to sound like "Rus/Russia" for use in this prophecy.

If "Rosh" means Russia, then the nations attacking Israel in this prophecy are led by Russia. If not, they are led by Turkey. Either way, Turkey is involved in the attack.

The other nations involved in the attack are easy to identify. Persia is the old name for Iran. The word the New King James translates "Ethiopia" is the Hebrew word "Cush" (כוש), which was a nation south of Egypt, covering parts of modern Sudan and Ethiopia. The word translated "Libya" is "Put" (פוט) in Hebrew, but there's no question that that's Libya. Gomer and Togarmah were also in modern Turkey. I don't think there's any serious mystery or disagreement about any of these.

6.15. Armageddon

Revelation 16:12, 16-21. Then the sixth angel poured out his bowl on the great river Euphrates, and its water was dried up, so that the way of the kings from the east might be prepared. ... And they gathered them together to the place called in Hebrew, Armageddon. Then the seventh angel poured out his bowl into the air, and a loud voice came out of the temple of heaven, from the throne, saying, "It is done!" And there were noises and thunderings and lightnings; and there was a great earthquake, such a mighty and great earthquake as had not occurred since men were on the earth. Now the great city was divided into three parts, and the cities of the nations fell. And great Babylon was remembered before God, to give her the cup of the wine of the fierceness of His wrath. Then every island fled away, and the mountains were not found. And great hail from heaven fell upon men, *each hailstone* about the weight of a talent. Men blasphemed God because of the plague of the hail, since that plague was exceedingly great.

There are (at least) two controversial questions here:
1. Is the Battle of Armageddon literal or figurative?
2. Is it something in the future, or in the past?

These verses mention four geographical places: the Euphrates River, the "east", Babylon, and of course, Armageddon.

The Euphrates is a real, literal river that runs through the modern nations of Turkey, Syria, and Iraq. It is the major river in the area. In the Old Testament, it was so prominent that it is often called simply "the River" (e.g. 2 Samuel 10:16, 1 Kings 4:21).

Babylon was a real city, though it no longer exists today. It was located about 50 miles south of modern Baghdad in Iraq. It went into decline about 300 BC and had long ceased to be an important city by the time Revelation was written circa AD 100. In AD 198 the Roman emperor Septimus Severus led an army conquering the region and reported that he found Babylon had been abandoned. People have lived among the ruins on and off since then.

When I say it no longer exists, I should make clear that I don't mean that it is totally erased from the Earth. There are ruins and archaeological excavations there, a small number of people live in the area, and when the region is at peace tourists visit the site. Sadam Hussein had plans to rebuild the city, but these were aborted by the Second Gulf War. After the war the U.S. had an army base there for a few years.

Christians routinely theorize that "Babylon" in Revelation is not the literal city of Babylon, but a symbol for some other place or idea. See section 6.24. An argument for it being the literal city is that here it is mentioned in connection with the Euphrates River, and the literal city of Babylon is on the Euphrates River – the river runs right through the middle of it.

"The east" is a little vague. In context it clearly means east of the Euphrates River. Of course that could mean any place from Persia to the Philippines. The Greek is literally "from the rising of the sun". This has led some people to theorize that it means Japan. The Japanese word for their country is "Nippon", which means "source of the sun", and which is often loosely translated "land of the rising sun". Note the identification sounds pretty strong in English translation: "rising of the sun" versus "land of the rising sun". But it's much less impressive if you take a more literal translation of the Japanese: "rising of the sun" versus "source of the sun". The only thing they have in common is the word "sun".

But most Christians today theorize that the "kings of the east" means China. If the Battle of Armageddon is literal and in the near future, this makes sense. China certainly has a powerful military. Some connect the "seven bowl judgements" of Revelation 16 with the "seven trumpet judgments" of Revelation 8-10. The sixth trumpet has some similarities to the sixth bowl:

> Revelation 9:13-16. Then the sixth angel sounded: And I heard a voice from the four horns of the golden altar which is before God, saying to the sixth angel who had the trumpet, "Release the four angels who are bound at the great river Euphrates." So the four angels, who had been prepared for the hour and day and month and year, were released to kill a third of mankind. Now the number of the army of the horsemen *was* two hundred million; I heard the number of them.

In both cases a powerful army is blocked by the Euphrates River, and then God removes the barrier. Back in the 1970s China announced that it had an army of 200 million men, and many Christians got quite excited about the match to the number in Revelation. Military analysts tended to dismiss the number as propaganda: Even a nation as big as China didn't have the population or the resources to maintain a standing army of 200 million. Rather, this was basically all the males of military age in the country. It was everyone who could theoretically be drafted in an extreme situation. Still, the government made the claim, and their claim matches the prophecy.

"Armageddon" is a Hebrew word meaning "hill" or "mountain" of Megiddo. Megiddo is a very large plain in northern Israel southwest of the Sea of Galilee. It was also the name for a town near the edge of that plain.

A number of battles have been fought there throughout history.

Pharaoh Thutmosis III fought the Syrians there in 1469 BC. This is said to be the first recorded battle in history, that is, the first battle of which we have any detailed historical records. Perhaps it is significant that Megiddo was the site of the first battle and will be the site of the last. Or maybe that's just an historical anomaly: people fought wars before 1469 BC, that's just the first battle that we know much about.

The Israelis under Joshua fought against the city of Megiddo circa 1400 BC. (Joshua 12:21) The Bible says that Joshua won the battle – read the verse, that's about all it says -- but apparently he didn't conquer Megiddo, or they later successfully revolted, because in the time of the judges they were independent. (Judges 1:27)

Egyptian records say that Schechem, an ally of Israel, attacked Megiddo. This was probably in the time of Joshua. Whether Schechem fought with Joshua against Megiddo or if this is a separate battle, I don't think anyone knows.

Gideon defeated the Midianites in the Valley of Jezreel, another name for the plain of Megiddo. (Judges 6:33)

Pharoah Shishak claimed to have destroyed the city circa 922 BC. It was later rebuilt, probably by King Ahab or King Omri.

King Josiah was killed in a battle there with Pharoah Necho. (2 Kings 23:29)

The Crusaders fought the Muslims there in AD 1099.

Napoleon defeated the Ottoman Turks there in 1799. He said, "All the armies of the world could maneuver their forces on this vast plain ... There is no place in the whole world more suited for war than this ... the most natural battleground of the whole earth".

British General Edmund Allenby defeated the Ottoman Turks there in 1918, driving them out of Palestine.

The reference to the "mountain of Megiddo" is not clear. We have no record of a mountain ever called Megiddo. The town is not on a mountain, and the plain is, well, a plain, not a mountain.

One theory is that this means Mount Carmel, which is near Megiddo. Mount Carmel was the place where Elijah challenged the prophets of Baal.

Another theory requires a little background: Ancient cities were often destroyed and rebuilt numerous times. They might be destroyed by invading armies, fires, or natural disasters. Or sections of a city might be demolished as part of a rebuilding project. Regardless of the manner of destruction, people flattened out the rubble and built new buildings on top of the remains of the old. So cities tended to rise, layer upon layer. Cities that were occupied for long periods of time turned into hills. These man-made hills are called "tel"s. Perhaps you have heard of the Israeli city of "Tel Aviv". So some say that "hill of Megiddo" here means "Tel Megiddo". The United Nations World Heritage Convention includes three tels in Israel on its "World Heritage List": Tel Hazor, Tel Beer Sheba, and Tel Megiddo. (http://whc.unesco.org/en/list/1108)

Futurists say that Revelation's description of the Battle of Armageddon refers to a literal, future battle. During the Great Tribulation an army from "the east", probably China, will come to attack Israel. The Euphrates River will be a challenging obstacle, but fortunately (from their point of view) the river will dry up. This may be a miracle, it may be a natural phenomenon, or the eastern army may divert or block the river. Whichever, they then make it to Megiddo where they attack the armies of Israel. Their army is then destroyed. Some believe they are defeated by Israel, perhaps aided by the U.S. or some other ally, and probably with nuclear weapons. Others say they are miraculously destroyed directly by God.

Futurists generally link Revelation 16 to Zechariah 14. I encourage you to read the whole chapter, but here's an excerpt:

Zechariah 14:1-4, 9, 12-13. A day of the LORD is coming, Jerusalem, when your possessions will be plundered and divided up within your very walls. I will gather all the nations to Jerusalem to fight against it; the city will be captured, the houses ransacked, and the women raped. Half of the city will go into exile, but the rest of the people will not be taken from the city. Then the LORD will go out and fight against those nations, as he fights on a day of battle. On that day his feet will stand on the Mount of Olives, east of Jerusalem, and the Mount of Olives will be split in two from east to west, forming a great valley, with half of the mountain moving north and half moving south. ... The LORD will be king over the whole earth. On that day there will be one LORD, and his name the only name. ... This is the plague with which the LORD will strike all the nations that fought against Jerusalem: Their flesh will rot while they are still standing on their feet, their eyes will rot in their sockets, and their tongues will rot in their mouths. On that day people will be stricken by the LORD with great panic. They will seize each other by the hand and attack one another.

Similarly, Ezekial 38:

Ezekiel 38:2-6. "Son of man, set your face against Gog, of the land of Magog, the prince of Rosh, Meshech, and Tubal, and prophesy against him, and say, 'Thus says the Lord GOD: "Behold, I *am* against you, O Gog, the prince of Rosh, Meshech, and Tubal. I will turn you around, put hooks into your jaws, and lead you out, with all your army, horses, and horsemen, all splendidly clothed, a great company *with* bucklers and shields, all of them handling swords. Persia, Ethiopia, and Libya are with them, all of them *with* shield and helmet; [6] Gomer and all its troops; the house of Togarmah *from* the far north and all its troops—many people *are* with you.

Ezekiel 38 says that the armies that attack Israel are led by "Gog of the land of Magog". As we discussed in section 6.14, Christians disagree about where Gog is from, and hence who leads this army. Basically, some say the army is led by people from the area of modern Turkey; others say it is led by Russia.

Modern commentators looking for a fulfillment of this prophecy in the near future – within the next few decades – tend to say that Magog must be Russia. Russia today is big and powerful and aggressive and a credible threat. Turkey is not particularly powerful militarily and has not been aggressive internationally – the last time that Turkey conquered foreign territory was the Polish-Ottoman War of 1672-1676. It's a lot easier, given present political realities, to imagine Russia deciding to invade the Middle East and attack Israel than it is to imagine Turkey attacking Israel. But this thinking might well be a trap. It's the trap of trying to fit Bible prophecies to current events, because it's much more interesting and exciting to say "this prophecy is being fulfilled before our eyes today" than "this prophecy was fulfilled by some ancient guy I never heard of thousands of years ago" or "this prophecy will be fulfilled by unknown people at some unknown time in the future". If the prophecy is not fulfilled until several hundred years from now, who knows what the political and military state of Russia and Turkey will be then?

Either way, Ezekiel 38 and Revelation 9 are probably not about the same battle. Ezekiel says the attack comes from "the far north", while Revelation 9 says the attack comes from "the east".

Preterists generally say that Revelation's discussion of the Battle of Armageddon refers to the fall of Jerusalem in AD 70.

There was no major battle in Megiddo during the Jewish War, though, so advocates of this theory have to say that the location is not literal. They have to say that somehow the plain of Megiddo, north of Jerusalem, is a symbol for the mountainous area of Jerusalem. The problem here is why John would have used Megiddo as a symbol for Jerusalem.

Also, the Roman army did not come from the east and did not cross the Euphrates River. Rome is west of Israel. The actual attack came from army bases north of Israel. The Romans were aided by Arabs from the south. That is, they came from every direction *except* the east.

Another theory, mostly held by Preterists, is that the Battle of Armageddon is not a literal battle, i.e. not really people lining up and trying to stab or shoot each other. Rather they say it is a symbolic description of the fight between Christianity and paganism.

They point out that some elements of the prophecy are clearly symbolic. The dragon and the beast are symbols described earlier in Revelation. The frogs coming out of their mouths are surely not literal. Babylon is probably a symbol and not the literal city. So it's plausible that the battle is not a literal battle.

As I noted above, there have been many battles fought at Megiddo. But if Revelation is talking about a literal battle, none of these historical battles really fit the description here. There has never been a case where an army from east of the Euphrates could not cross the river, and the river then dried up, either in a natural or miraculous way, and they were able to pass to reach Megiddo and fight a battle. So if this passage is literal, it would seem it must be in the future.

The battle described in Ezekiel 38 doesn't end well for Gog.

Ezekiel 38:17-23. 'This is what the Sovereign LORD says: You are the one I spoke of in former days by my servants the prophets of Israel. At that time they prophesied for years that I would bring you against them. This is what will happen in that day: When Gog attacks the land of Israel, my hot anger will be aroused, declares the Sovereign LORD. In my zeal and fiery wrath I declare that at that time there shall be a great earthquake in the land of Israel. The fish in the sea, the birds in the sky, the beasts of the field, every creature that moves along the ground, and all the people on the face of the earth will tremble at my presence. The mountains will be overturned, the cliffs will crumble and every wall will fall to the ground. I will summon a sword against Gog on all my mountains, declares the Sovereign LORD. Every man's sword will be against his brother. I will execute judgment on him with plague and bloodshed; I will pour down torrents of rain, hailstones and burning sulfur on him and on his troops and on the many nations with him. And so I will show my greatness and my holiness, and I will make myself known in the sight of many nations. Then they will know that I am the LORD.'

Many modern Futurists interpret the descriptions of the destruction of the invading army as a nuclear attack. "A great earthquake … mountains will be overturned, the cliffs will crumble" could describe megaton bombs being dropped. "Their flesh will rot while they are still standing on their feet, their eyes will rot in their sockets, and their tongues will rot in their mouths" are graphic but accurate descriptions of what happens to people caught in the blast of a nuclear bomb.

But there's a problem trying to put Ezekiel 38 in the future. Ezekiel says that the invading army will be riding horses and armed with swords and shields (verses 4 and 15). Surely a 21st century army would not give up its tanks and guns and attack on horseback with swords.

Some advocates of a literal battle reply that Ezekiel also says, "Thus says the Lord God … I will turn you around, put hooks into your jaws, and lead you out," Clearly the hooks in Gog's mouth are not literal, but rather a figurative way of saying that God will lead Gog to make this attack that turns out to be suicidal. If the hooks are figurative, perhaps the swords and shields are also figurative. But read Ezekiel 38:2-6 carefully. It talks about swords and horses and shields over and over, as if the writer really wants to emphasize that these are the weapons used.

It is, perhaps, interesting to note that Zechariah does not mention any specific weapons. His prophecy could be applicable to an army of any era.

6.16. Israel

The Romans virtually destroyed Israel after the Bar Kokhba Revolt in AD 134. 600,000 Jews were killed, and many more exiled or enslaved. Jews were barred from entering Jerusalem, which the Romans renamed Aelia Capitolina. The temple had been destroyed in the AD 70 revolt. Now the Romans built a temple to Jupiter on the site, with statues of Jupiter and the Emperor Hadrian. The Romans even merged the provinces of

Judaea and Syria together and called it "Syria Palaestina", to eliminate the name "Judaea" from the map. The name "Judaea" came from the name of the southern Jewish kingdom of Judah, after Israel was divided in two following the reign of Solomon. (1 Kings 12.)

The Romans were trying to eradicate all record of Israel. While there were still Jews in the world, there was no "nation of Israel", not even as a client state under the thumb of the Romans.

This created a problem for interpretation of Bible prophecy by Christians for millennia. There were many references to Israel in prophecy that had not yet been fulfilled.

For example:

Amos 9:13-15. "Behold, the days are coming," says the LORD, "When ... I will bring back the captives of My people Israel; They shall build the waste cities and inhabit *them;* They shall plant vineyards and drink wine from them; They shall also make gardens and eat fruit from them. I will plant them in their land, And no longer shall they be pulled up From the land I have given them," Says the LORD your God.

While Israel has been destroyed and re-created several times, none of those restorations could be the fulfillment of this prophecy, because it ends by saying that "no longer shall they be pulled up from the land". In AD 134 they *were* pulled up again.

Similarly, Zechariah 12 describes a great war against Israel. No one could connect this to any war fought in the past, so it must be a prophecy for the future. But how could there be a future war against Israel, when there was no longer an Israel?

Christians came up with two theories:

Theory 1: Israel would somehow be restored in the future. As time went on this theory seemed more and more unlikely. The old land of Israel was conquered by Muslims, who hated the Jews. They seemed extremely unlikely to allow the Jews to carve out an independent country in Muslim-controlled territory.

Theory 2: The Christian Church took the place of Israel in

prophecy. That is, prophecies about Israel would be fulfilled in the Church.

The theory that the Church replaced Israel in prophecy is sometimes called "Replacement Theology" – mostly by its opponents – and sometimes called Covenant Theology. The theory that Israel literally means Israel is called Dispensation Theology.

Scriptures given to support Covenant Theology include:

Romans 2:28-29. For he is not a Jew who *is one* outwardly, nor *is* circumcision that which *is* outward in the flesh; but *he is* a Jew who *is one* inwardly; and circumcision *is that* of the heart, in the Spirit, not in the letter; whose praise *is* not from men but from God.

Circumcision was the outward, physical symbol that one was a Jew. Paul says here that just because one has the outward symbol doesn't make him a true Jew, that is, a true follower of God.

Phillipians 3:3. For we are the circumcision, who worship God in the Spirit, rejoice in Christ Jesus, and have no confidence in the flesh.

Those who have faith in Christ are the "real" circumcision.

Romans 9:6-8. But it is not that the word of God has taken no effect. For they *are* not all Israel who *are* of Israel, nor *are they* all children because they are the seed of Abraham; but, "In Isaac your seed shall be called." That is, those who *are* the children of the flesh, these *are* not the children of God; but the children of the promise are counted as the seed.

So those who are descended from Abraham and who have been circumcised are not necessarily God's chosen people. God's chosen people are those who trust in God and obey his commands. Israel broke the covenant they had made with God. So God finally abandoned them and created a new chosen people, the Church.

Scriptures to support Dispensation Theology include:

Romans 11:1-5. I say then, has God cast away His people? Certainly not! For I also am an Israelite, of the seed of Abraham, *of* the tribe of Benjamin. God has not cast away His people whom He foreknew. Or do you not know what the Scripture says of Elijah, how he pleads with God against Israel, saying, "LORD, they have killed Your prophets and torn down Your altars, and I alone am left, and they seek my life"? But what does the divine response say to him? "I have reserved for Myself seven thousand men who have not bowed the knee to Baal." Even so then, at this present time there is a remnant according to the election of grace.

Yes, Israel has turned away from God. But God has not abandoned Israel. God has always maintained a faithful remnant in Israel.

Romans 11:25-27. For I do not desire, brethren, that you should be ignorant of this mystery, lest you should be wise in your own opinion, that blindness in part has happened to Israel until the fullness of the Gentiles has come in. And so all Israel will be saved, as it is written: "The Deliverer will come out of Zion, And He will turn away ungodliness from Jacob; For this *is* My covenant with them, When I take away their sins."

Israel has turned its back on God. God is now giving the Gentiles an opportunity to become his people. But he has not forgotten Israel, and when the Gentiles' time is complete, God will restore Israel.

Revelation 7:4-5. And I heard the number of those who were sealed. One hundred *and* forty-four thousand of all the tribes of the children of Israel *were* sealed: Of the tribe of Judah twelve thousand *were* sealed; of the tribe of Reuben twelve thousand *were* sealed; of the tribe of Gad twelve thousand *were* sealed; …

He goes on to list all twelve tribes. If "Israel" now means "the Church", then what does it mean to list the twelve tribes? This seems very specific for a metaphor.

Side note: Curiously, the list of the twelve tribes in Revelation 7 is not quite the same as the list in the Old Testament. The twelve tribes were named after Jacob's twelve sons. But in Revelation, one son, Dan, is missing. In his place is Manasseh, one of Joseph's sons, i.e. a grandson of Jacob. But Joseph is still there in the list. There is no explanation for this substitution. Some theorize that Dan is excluded because the tribe of Dan will betray their fellow Jews, or engage in some great sin. Personally, I wonder if this isn't just a matter of historical reality: the tribe of Dan dies out.

Advocates of Dispensation Theology say that the idea that God's promises to Israel will now be fulfilled in the Church would mean that God is breaking his promises to Israel. "Fulfilling" a promise to a different person than the one you promised it to isn't fulfilling it at all. If your insurance company promised to pay for repairs if you were in an accident, and then when the time came they refused to give you the money, and the insurance agent explained, "I decided to give that money to my brother-in-law instead", would you say that the insurance company had lived up to its promises? Surely not. How could a holy God break his promises like that?

The original problem that led to Covenant Theology was that Israel no longer existed as a nation. But this problem went away in 1948 when Israel was re-created after almost 2000 years.

In my opinion, Covenant Theology is based on a lack of faith. The Bible said that certain things would happen to Israel. People couldn't see how those prophecies could possibly be fulfilled, and so they concluded that they had to come up with some "work around" to explain how they could be fulfilled in a non-literal way.

Isaac Newton invented calculus, discovered the theory of gravity, formulated the Three Laws of Motion, invented the reflecting telescope, and made numerous other contributions to science and mathematics. Many scientists consider him the greatest scientist who ever lived.

He was also a Bible-believing Christian. He wrote a book, *History of the Ancient Kingdoms*, defending the Bible from atheist attacks of his day.

He also wrote a book about the prophecies of Daniel and Revelation in the early 1700s. Regarding Israel, he wrote:

> And lastly, that this rebuilding of Jerusalem and the waste places of Judah is predicted in Mic 7:11, Amos 9:11, 14, Ezek 36:33, 35, 36, 38, Isa 54:3, 11, 12, 55:12, 61:4, 65:18, 21, 22, and Tobit 14:5, and that the return from captivity and coming of the Messiah and his kingdom are described in Daniel 7, Rev 19, Acts 1, Mat 24, Joel 3, Ezek 36, 37, Isa 55, 57, 58, 65, and 66, and many other places of scripture. The manner I know not. Let time be the interpreter.

>   – Isaac Newton, *Observations Upon the Prophecies of Daniel and the Apocalypse of St John*, chapter 10

Newton recognized the problem: How could these prophecies be fulfilled when Israel no longer existed? In his time it seemed totally impossible. But instead of trying to re-interpret scripture to accommodate current events, he concluded that somehow – "the manner I know not" – the prophecies would be fulfilled just like God said.

Now, 300 years after Newton, we see that God did indeed fulfill the prophecies exactly like he said he would.

I think the example of Israel is a good one to keep in mind when we discuss Bible prophecy. Yes, there are many prophecies that are not intended to be taken literally. In some cases, like Daniel's prophecy about the statue, we are clearly told that this is symbolic and not literal. But if we find ourselves saying, "Well, it sounds like it's meant literally, but it can't be because I just don't see how it could happen that way" ... I think we should step back and rethink. If God wants it to happen that way, who are you or I to say that he cannot make it happen? Maybe the prophecy doesn't make sense if we suppose it will happen in our own time -- but it won't be fulfilled for another 500 years. Or maybe it doesn't make sense within this grand theory that we have built -- but our theory is wrong.

Advocates of Covenant Theology say that it's not *just* to explain away the non-existence of Israel, that the theory also explains other things in scripture. See the verses I listed above in defense of Covenant Theology.

6.17. Seven Churches

The book of Revelation is specifically addressed to seven churches. It begins with a special message for each of these churches.

> Revelation 1:9-11. I, John, both your brother and companion in the tribulation and kingdom and patience of Jesus Christ, was on the island that is called Patmos for the word of God and for the testimony of Jesus Christ. I was in the Spirit on the Lord's Day, and I heard behind me a loud voice, as of a trumpet, saying, "I am the Alpha and the Omega, the First and the Last," and, "What you see, write in a book and send it to the seven churches which are in Asia: to Ephesus, to Smyrna, to Pergamos, to Thyatira, to Sardis, to Philadelphia, and to Laodicea."

Chapters 2 and 3 are the messages for each of the churches. I encourage you to read Revelation chapters 1 through 3. I can't quote three entire chapters here.

The letters all follow a consistent pattern. They all begin, "These things says ..." followed by a description of Jesus that relates to other things in the book of Revelation. Then they say, "I know your works", followed by praise for the church. (Except Laodicea, for which he has no praise.) Then, "But I have this against you", followed by criticism. (Except Smyrna, for which he has no criticism.) Then, "To him who overcomes" and a promise of reward for those who do well. There is some variation in the exact words of each "lead in", and your Bible may translate it differently.

Each of the letters is addressed, not to the church itself,

but to the "angel" of the church. Who are these angels?

Theory 1: God appointed an angel to watch over each of these churches. Some conclude there is an angel assigned to every church.

Theory 2: The word translated "angels", here and throughout the New Testament, is the Greek word ΑΓΓΕΛΟΙ ("aggeloi"). Aggeloi literally means simply "messengers". There are a handful of places in the Bible where it is used to refer to ordinary humans, and in these it is usually translated "messengers". For example, in Luke 7:24 the messengers sent to Jesus by John the Baptist are called aggeloi. James 2:25 refers to the spies that Joshua sent to Jericho as aggeloi. When aggeloi refers to spiritual beings who God uses as messengers, it is translated "angels". You may note that most occurrences of the word "angel" in the New Testament are in the phrase "angel of the Lord" or "angel of God". This might seem redundant if you don't know the Greek word. Angel "of God" as opposed to what? An angel of my neighbor down the street? But in fact that's exactly why the Bible uses this phrase. In Greek, we need to distinguish between "a messenger from my neighbor" and "a messenger from God".

So some say that the angels/messengers of Revelation 1 through 3 are not spiritual beings but humans, the pastors of these churches. In context this makes sense. Why would God ask John to write letters to angels? How would John deliver a letter to an angel? But if we understand this to mean "the messenger of the church", i.e. the pastor or some other leader, then God telling a prophet to give them a message makes a lot of sense, and is exactly how God worked elsewhere in the Bible.

By the way, to the best of my knowledge, Revelation 1-3 is the only place in the Bible where it's not clear if the word "aggeloi" is referring to spiritual beings or humans.

There are three theories about the identity or significance of the churches themselves.

Theory 1: They are seven literal, specific churches that existed in John's time.

Theory 2: They represent seven types of churches that will exist throughout history.

Theory 3: This is a prophecy of seven church ages, characteristics that the Church of that age as a whole will have, beginning with John's time and down to the Second Coming.

These are routinely presented as three contrasting theories. But it is possible that any combination of them could be true. They could all be true.

Number one can be proven true. By "Asia" here John means, not the continent of Asia as we think of it today, but the Roman province called Asia, which is mostly the same area as the modern nation of Turkey, sometimes called "Asia Minor".

The seven cities that John lists are real cities that existed in Asia during his lifetime. All seven cities are mentioned in surviving books written by ancient Greeks and Romans.

About 140 BC Antipater of Sidon made a list of what he called the "Seven Wonders of the World". You've probably heard the phrase even if you can't list them. One of them was the Temple of Artemis in Ephesus. The book of Acts mentions this temple, Acts 19:21-41, and how a man who sold souvenirs to tourists who visited the temple stirred up trouble against Christians, because this new religion threatened his business – trouble that ended with a riot. (Many English translations say "Diana" rather than "Artemis". The original Greek says Artemis, which is the Greek name of the goddess. The Romans called her Diana.) The book of Ephesians was written to the church in Ephesus. Jesus's mother Mary spent the last years of her life in Ephesus and may have died there.

A stadium seating 20,000 people was built in Smyrna for Olympic games. 50 years after Revelation was written, the early church leader Polycarp was killed in this stadium.

Pergamos was the capitol of the region. It was also known

as the home of a library with over 200,000 books, at the time the second largest library in the world, second only to the Library of Alexandria.

Thyatira was famous for producing dyes to make colorful clothes.

Alexander the Great commissioned a temple to Zeus to be built in Sardis. Apparently the Jewish influence in Sardis was strong, because archaeologists have found the remains of a large Jewish synagogue.

The word "Philadelphia" is Greek for "brotherly love". According to Greek historians, the city was named to honor the loyalty of Attalus to his older brother Eumenes, king of Pergamos. At one point Eumenes disappeared and was thought to be dead, so Attalus took the throne. When Eumenes turned out to be alive and returned, Attalus stepped down voluntarily. Later, the Romans decided that they didn't like Eumenes and offered to help Attalus overthrow his brother and become king. He turned them down. Attalus did eventually become king when his brother died for real. The American city of Philadelphia is named after this city.

Laodicea was a famous banking center in ancient times. It has been called "the Wall Street of Asia". When Asia became a Roman province, the Roman governor's home was in Laodicea. When the city was badly damaged by an earthquake in AD 61, Rome offered "disaster relief" to help rebuild. Laodicea rejected the offer and paid to rebuild the city themselves.

And so on. Ancient histories say many things about all these cities.

The point of this little travelogue is that these were real, literal cities, and there were real, literal Christian churches in each of them.

The locations of all seven are known to archaeologists today and have been excavated. Six of the seven cities are still inhabited. Ephesus is still called Ephesus; Smyrna is now called Izmir; Pergamos is now Bergama; Thyatira is now Akhisar; Sardis is now Sard; Philadelphia is now Alasehir. Only Laodicea is uninhabited. While using the Internet to research this chapter I came across several travel companies that will take you on a tour of all seven sites.

So were these seven literal churches that existed in John's time? Yes. There is no question about that.

The seven churches also represent different types of churches. Read each of the letters and you see that each church has a distinctive "personality". Bible commentators have long referred to them by shorthand descriptions. Not that all commentators have used exactly the same words, but they are generally very similar. The New King James uses the following section heads – note not part of the inspired text, but added by modern commentators:

Ephesus:	The Loveless Church
Smyrna:	The Persecuted Church
Pergamos:	The Compromising Church
Thyatira:	The Corrupt Church
Sardis:	The Dead Church
Philadelphia:	The Faithful Church
Laodicea:	The Lukewarm Church

Most of these titles are negative, but Jesus had both criticism and praise for each of the seven churches. (Except, as noted above, there is no praise for Laodicea and no criticism for Smyrna.)

There have obviously been churches throughout history and down to today that fit the "template" of each of these churches. There have always been churches that were loveless, churches that were persecuted, etc. So in that sense, it is clearly true that these churches can be thought of as "types".

On the other hand, some elements of the descriptions are very specific. For example, Thyatira is criticized "because you allow that woman Jezebel, who calls herself a prophetess, to teach and seduce My servants to commit sexual immorality and eat things sacrificed to idols" (Revelation 2:20) Are there any churches today that have a woman member named Jezebel who calls herself a prophetess, etc? Probably not. Even if we assume that "Jezebel" is not her actual name but a reference to the Old Testament queen (1 Kings 16 – 2 Kings 9), or that the specific name is not the point, how many churches today have an issue with eating things sacrificed to idols?

Few churches today would fit every element of the description of any one of the seven churches.

Even if we ignore some of the details, it's not clear that thinking of these as seven types gives an exhaustive list, that is, that every church in history would fit one and exactly one of these descriptions. There are some classification systems that cover all possibilities. Like if we divide numbers into odd and even, every integer is one or the other. There are no other alternatives. You can divide it by two, or you can't. But these descriptions do not clearly cover all possibilities nor are they mutually exclusive. Couldn't a church be compromising and also be lukewarm? Couldn't there be a church that is not loveless, not persecuted, etc, that doesn't meet any of these?

Nowhere does Revelation say that this is an exhaustive and mutually exclusive list of types. Perhaps the point is just to say, Here are strengths and weaknesses that these seven particular churches had, and that your church might (or might not) have, and you would be wise to learn from it. But at that point, it's just like many other Bible stories: people long ago did such-and-such, and the story is included in the Bible because people throughout history can learn from it. Christians don't normally suppose that all leaders can be divided into the Saul-type or the David-type or the Solomon-type. But we can certainly learn from the strengths and weaknesses of these three kings.

So have there been churches throughout history that have fit into these seven types? If we ignore some of the details and just consider them as very general types, surely yes. Does every church that has ever existed fit in one and only one of these seven types? Probably not.

The third theory is that the seven churches represent seven church ages. While details vary, most advocates of this theory map out the seven ages as in Figure 1.

Figure 1		
Revelation Church	**Beginning Year**	**Age**
Ephesus	30	Apostolic age
Smyrna	100	Persecution under the Caesars
Pergamos	312	Official religion of Roman Empire
Thyatira	600	Rise of Catholic Church
Sardis	1517	Reformation
Philadelphia	1750	Great Awakening, missionary age
Laodicea	1900	Theological liberalism and decadence

Most sources I have found give these same basic eras, There is some variation on the dates and details, but I think the above is fairly typical.

I wondered about the starting dates given to each era. I found it was surprisingly difficult to find how various versions of the theory came up with their dates. While many books and web sites list the dates, few say why they picked a particular year, and I couldn't find any that gave a clear and complete list.

Most versions of this theory start the Ephesus Age either with Jesus's crucifixion or with the founding of one of the early churches.

I found none that gave a specific event to start the Smyrna Age. I would have chosen the persecution under Nero, the first serious, violent persecution by Rome, AD 66. But most gave dates between AD 100 and AD 200.

The Pergamos Era was simple and consistent. Almost all advocates of this theory start it with the Roman emperor Constantine. They varied a little on the exact date: Some took the year Constantine converted to Christianity, AD 312; or the next year when he officially legalized Christianity; or the Council of Nicaea, when the government got involved in deciding Church doctrine, AD 325; or when Christianity was declared the official religion of the empire, AD 380.

I found one source that said the Thyatira Era began with the election of Pope Gregory in AD 590, who was one of the most successful popes. The Protestant reformer John Calvin said that Gregory was "the last good pope". Others put the start of Thyatira 10 or 20 years later, but I'm not sure what they're pinning that date on.

The Sardis Age is another easy one: almost all advocates of the theory begin Sardis on the date when Martin Luther began the Protestant Reformation by nailing his 95 Theses to the door of the Wittenberg Church, AD 1517.

I found no explanation for the common dates to start the Philadelphia Age. 1750 is often given. This is the year that Jonathan Edwards began the First Great Awakening, so maybe that's where it comes from. Others give dates scattered through the 1700s and 1800s.

The most variation probably comes for Laodicea, but most give dates from the late 1800s or early 1900s. I found no source that gave a specific event for their chosen starting date.

As I was writing this chapter, I considered not mentioning my inability to find events for the specific dates, for fear that I was confessing to inadequate research! Frankly, I am not sure if the problem is that, (a) I just didn't look hard enough; (b) The people who advocate this theory failed to spell out the details in their books and sermons for some unknown reason; or (c) They don't always have a specific event to start an era. Maybe the idea is just "somewhere around AD 1750 this sort of thing started happening".

This theory is essentially a Protestant theory. It is unlikely that a Catholic would describe the era of the greatest power of the Catholic Church as a time of corruption.

One can certainly find some elements of the letters to the

churches that closely match these eras.

Ephesus is praised for testing people who claim to be apostles and distinguishing true preachers from false preachers. And indeed this was a challenge that faced the early church. Before the New Testament was written and assembled, Christians had no authoritative guide to correct doctrine.

Smyrna is described as a persecuted church. The church certainly was persecuted under the Caesars, when thousands of Christians were tortured and killed for their faith. It also describes them struggling with "those who say they are Jews and are not", perhaps a reference to people who were Jews by birth but rejected Jesus as the Messiah.

Pergamos is warned that they were "living where Satan's throne is", and that there were people among them who were compromising with worldly powers. Under Constantine, Christianity became the official religion of the Roman Empire. So now the "headquarters" of Christianity was in Rome, which just a few years before had been the center of pagan worship. The church now had the ear of the emperor, and so there was a temptation to politicize the faith. The power of the government was called in to enforce compliance with "correct" doctrine.

The major issue with Thyatira is that they have a woman who is a leader in the church who is leading people into sexual immorality. Thyatira is the age of the Catholic Church. It's difficult to identify any literal woman who can be identified with this "Jezebel": even if we ignore the name, what woman was a leader in the Catholic Church who led people into sexual immorality? Perhaps we could say that Jezebel is not an actual person, but rather a symbol for a "trend". Then, yes, there were priests and popes who were sexually immoral, but is this really the defining characteristic of the Catholic era? There's no mention of the growing political power and wealth of the church. Protestants see this as a time when the Catholic Church became corrupt. (And many Catholics concede there were problems that demanded reform.) But there's no mention of anything like this in the description of Thyatira.

Sardis is told that they have a "reputation for being alive, but you are dead", and that there are "a few people who have not defiled their clothes". This could be taken as a description of the Reformation. The Church appeared to be strong and vibrant because it was rich and politically powerful, but it had lost track of its original purpose: preaching the Gospel. Fortunately there is a faithful remnant. Except, nowhere does it say that this remnant would reform the Church or break away and start over, it just says that they exist within the Church. The letter to Sardis sort of fits, but not obviously so.

Philadelphia is congratulated for "enduring" even though they "have little strength". But the Church of the 18th and 19th centuries did much more than "endure". It was a time of the greatest growth the Church has ever seen. Missionaries were sent all over the world. The Church was rich and politically powerful, but unlike under Constantine and the popes, there was little trouble with corruption. (Not none, of course.) Philadelphia is also warned about "those who claim to be Jews but are not", like Smyrna. How was that an issue in the 19th century, in a way that it had not been since AD 300?

Laodicea is told that they are "lukewarm", neither hot nor cold. They think they are rich and have everything they need but they are "pitiful", "blind", and "naked". That seems an apt description of the 20th and 21st century Western church. It is rich and comfortable, but it has compromised with the world. It hasn't abandoned the Gospel – it's not "cold" – but it doesn't boldly preach the Gospel either – it's not "hot". It is rich in material things but poor in spirit.

So okay, five of the seven seem to fit the assigned ages fairly well. And presumably one could come up with interpretations to make the other two fit.

But there are other catches.

One: Imagine this little experiment. Write the descriptions on index cards, shuffle them, and give them to someone who knows history very well but doesn't remember the order the letters appear in Revelation. Then ask him to map these descriptions to church ages. Do you think that he would obviously and inevitably get it right? Laodicea, the lukewarm church, could describe the time under Constantine or the popes just as well as it describes the modern Church. Philadelphia, the faithful church, describes the Church under the Caesars better than it describes the 19th century: they were poor and weak but managed to endure. The sexual immorality of Thyatira describes the 21st century Church very well, with its growing acceptance of divorce, abortion, and homosexuality. Ephesus's "you do good works but have lost your first love" is at least as good a description of the Catholic Church of the Middle Ages as of the Apostolic Age. Etc.

Two: This theory is very Western-centric. At best it describes the history of the Church in Europe and North America. An African or Asian person reading these descriptions would find little relevance to his own history. For example, while the 21st century Church in Europe can well be described as "Laodicean" -- rich and comfortable and lukewarm -- this is pretty much the opposite of the state of the 21st century Church in China or Iran. They would be much more readily identified with Smyrna, the persecuted church.

Three: If we sum up the letters to each of the churches into headlines, "The Persecuted Church", etc, these can be mapped fairly well to eras of Church history. But the details often don't match. Several letters mention the teaching of the "Nicolaitans". No one today knows who these people were or what they taught.

By the way, I've seen some fanciful theories of who the Nicolaitans were based on the root words in the name. They say it comes from a word meaning "ruler" or "conquerer" and another meaning "the people" or "the laity", so the Nicolaitans were "rulers of the people". From there they speculate that this was a group that tried to make themselves rulers of the church. But it's not at all clear that there is any significance to the etymology of the name. Like, the name "Napoleon" literally means "of the new city". Would it therefore be fair to conclude that the Napoleonic Era was all about building new cities? It's quite likely the Nicolaitans were simply named after the person who started the movement, and that what his parents were thinking when they named him has nothing to do with his movement. Even if we accept that this group gave themselves this name as a description, or that their opponents gave them this name, it's still far too vague to tell us anything. Who were they trying to rule or conquer, rule in what way, and why?

The letter to Pergamos mentions a member of the church named Antipas being martyred. Antipas was a pastor in Pergamos who was martyred in AD 92. This was shortly before the book of Revelation was written, and so would be a very likely thing to bring up in a letter to the literal church of Pergamos. But it was over 200 years before the start of the "Pergamos Age".

Thyatira is told to "hold on to what you have until I come". Sardis is told "I will come upon you as a thief, and you will not know what hour I will come upon you". Philadelphia is told, "I am coming quickly". These appear to be references to the Second Coming. But these three Church Ages are supposed to end well before the Second Coming. And Laodicea, the age when the Second Coming is supposed to happen, doesn't have any clear mention of Christ's return.

And so on. There are a number of references to people and issues that were relevant to the literal seven churches in Asia, that are difficult to interpret as having relevance to Church ages.

This theory is fairly recent. As I said in the introduction, my purpose in this book is not to trace the history of each theory, but in this case its helpful to know a little of the history to understand the theory. The earliest references to this theory I can find are from Josiah Litch and Uriah Smith in the 1840s. These men were part of a movement that eventually became the Seventh Day Adventist Church. They put the Era of Laodicea beginning in their own time. The theory was popularized by William Branham in the 1950s. Branham was a faith healer who taught that when Revelation speaks of the "angel" or "messenger" of each of the seven churches, this meant the foremost spiritual leader of each age. And Branham said that the messenger of the seventh church age was Branham. Search the internet for "seven church ages" and most of the links you find will be to Branham's version of the theory, but they usually don't list Branham as the seventh messenger. Herbert Armstrong taught a version of this theory in the 1970s, though he put Sardis beginning in 1933 and Philadelphia beginning with himself. Armstrong founded the Worldwide Church of God.

If this was the meaning of these chapters in Revelation, why did no one notice it for 1700 years? I can't find any record of someone in, say, AD 1000 saying, "Oh, look, we are presently in the fourth Church age, so there are three more still to come."

I am trying to be fair to the Seven Church Ages theory. I used to believe it, but the more I have studied the question, the less plausible it sounds to me.

6.18. Dragon

Revelation talks about a dragon in four places: 12:1-12, 13:1-4, briefly in 16:13, and 20:1-4, 7-10. I won't quote all of that here, but just to give some excerpts:

Revelation 12:3-9. And another sign appeared in heaven: behold, a great, fiery red dragon having seven heads and ten horns, and seven diadems on his heads. His tail drew a third of the stars of heaven and threw them to the earth. And the dragon stood before the woman who was ready to give birth, to devour her Child as soon as it was born. She bore a male Child who was to rule all nations with a rod of iron. And her Child was caught up to God and His throne. Then the woman fled into the wilderness, where she has a place prepared by God, that they should feed her there one thousand two hundred and sixty days. And war broke out in heaven: Michael and his angels fought with the dragon; and the dragon and his angels fought, but they did not prevail, nor was a place found for them in heaven any longer. So the great dragon was cast out, that serpent of old, called the Devil and Satan, who deceives the whole world; he was cast to the earth, and his angels were cast out with him.

Revelation 13:1-2, 4. Then I stood on the sand of the sea. And I saw a beast rising up out of the sea, having seven heads and ten horns, and on his horns ten crowns, and on his heads a blasphemous name. Now the beast which I saw was like a leopard, his feet were like *the feet of* a bear, and his mouth like the mouth of a lion. The dragon gave him his power, his throne, and great authority. … So they worshiped the dragon who gave authority to the beast; and they worshiped the beast, saying, "Who *is* like the beast? Who is able to make war with him?"

Revelation 20:1-2. Then I saw an angel coming down from heaven, having the key to the bottomless pit and a great chain in his hand. He laid hold of the dragon, that serpent of old, who is *the* Devil and Satan, and bound him for a thousand years;

Revelation 20:7-10. Now when the thousand years have expired, Satan will be released from his prison and will go out to deceive the nations which are in the four corners of the earth, Gog and Magog, to gather them together to battle, whose number *is* as the sand of the sea. They went up on the breadth of the earth and surrounded the camp of the saints and the beloved city. And fire came down from God out of heaven and devoured them. The devil, who deceived them, was cast into the lake of fire and brimstone where the beast and the false prophet *are*. And they will be tormented day and night forever and ever.

The plain reading here is that the Dragon is Satan. Revelation 12:9 explicitly says that the Dragon is "called the Devil, and Satan", and 20:2 says "the dragon … who is the Devil and Satan".

Nevertheless, many commentators say that the Dragon is the Roman Empire.

Generally, their position is that the Dragon *primarily* symbolizes Satan, but *secondarily* symbolizes Rome.

There are basically two reasons for this.

One: Chapter 12 tells us that the Dragon attempts to kill the "child". The child is usually understood to be Christ – see section 6.23. So the Dragon must be the forces that tried to kill Christ. It was a Roman governor, Pilate, who officially ordered Christ's crucifixion and Roman soldiers who carried out the execution. So they identify the dragon with Rome.

But the Bible says that the Dragon attempted to "devour her Child as soon as it was born", Revelation 12:4. The crucifixion was 30-some years later. It was Herod who tried to kill Jesus as soon as he was born, and the Bible doesn't mention the Romans having anything to do with that.

In any case, Satan was presumably behind both the failed attempt to kill Jesus as a baby and the successful attempt to kill him as an adult. (Successful in the sense that he was indeed killed. Presumably Satan did not expect the Resurrection. Oops.) We don't need to suppose that the dragon is a "dual symbol" to make sense of the story. It makes perfect sense if we understand the dragon to be Satan as the text says, and, sure, he works through human agents such as Herod and Pilate.

Two: There are parallels between the description of the Dragon and the Fourth Beast of Daniel 7. Or at least, one key parallel: the Fourth Beast of Daniel has 10 horns, and so does the Dragon of Revelation.

Some also point out that combined, the four beasts of Daniel have a total of 7 heads and 10 horns, matching the Dragon of Revelation. As the Roman Empire conquered the three earlier empires, it absorbed the additional heads.

Personally I think this is a stretch.

There are four beasts. There is no mention of how many heads three of them have, which presumably means the conventional one each. The third beast has four heads. So 1 + 1 + 4 + 1 = 7 heads. There is no mention of the first three beasts having horns. They are "like a lion", "like a bear", and "like a leopard", animals that don't have horns, so it's fair to suppose the first three had no horns. The fourth beast has 10 horns. So 0 + 0 + 0 + 10 = 10. Thus 7 heads and 10 horns.

The beasts of Daniel 7 are normally identified as Babylon, Persia, Greece (under Alexander the Great), and Rome. The four heads of the third beast are routinely interpreted to refer to the fact that when Alexander died, his empire was divided into four parts under four separate rulers. But Alexander conquered Babylon and Persia, so by the "absorbed" theory, the Third Beast had a total of 6 heads. Which would then make the prophecy false, because Alexander's empire broke into 4 pieces, not 6. And Rome never conquered Babylon or Persia and only conquered about half of what had been Alexander's Empire, so Rome could only have "absorbed" 2 or maybe 3 of the former empires' heads. This argument for the theory just doesn't hold up.

The Dragon has some parallels to the beast or beasts of chapters 13 and 17. (See section 6.19.) Revelation 13 says that the Beast has 10 horns. Some ancient manuscripts also say "7 heads", others don't include this.

Side note: You often hear anti-Christians say that it's impossible to know the original text of the Bible because it has been copied and translated so many times. They'll talk about how there are hundreds of thousands of discrepancies between manuscripts. This is mostly bogus. Yes, there are, by some counts, 200,000 discrepancies between ancient Bible manuscripts. But to get this number you have to count every copy of every manuscript. We have over 24,000 ancient copies of the Bible. If in those 24,000 copies, 13,000 say X and 11,000 say Y, they count that as 11,000 discrepancies. Compare this to the next richest ancient text, Homer's Iliad. We have 643 copies of the Iliad. The fact that we have so many copies of the Bible that are almost identical is used as evidence *against* the accuracy of the Bible. If you count discrepancies per copy, then the more copies you have, the more discrepancies, which isn't really a fair measure of the number of problems. If you just count the number of places where there is a difference between any pair of ancient manuscripts, there are more like 10,000 discrepancies. Still sounds like a lot, except that almost all of those are changes in spelling over time or between regions, like the difference between "sulfur" and "sulphur" in English, or are simple spelling errors, like a letter left out when copying. There are about 400 words in the New Testament that are actually in question. The "seven heads" are two of them.

Chapter 17 also describes a beast with 7 heads and 10 horns. This may or may not be the same beast as chapter 13.

The Beast of Revelation 13 is clearly not the same being as the Dragon. Revelation 13:2 says, "the dragon gave him his power", and 13:4 says, "So they worshiped the dragon who gave authority to the beast; and they worshiped the beast". These are two different beings.

Most commentators say that the Beast of Revelation 17 is the same entity as the Beast of Revelation 13. (See section 6.19.) Both the Beast of Revelation 17 and the Dragon have 7 heads and 10 horns, but that is the only real similarity between them. The Beast is never called a "dragon" and the Dragon is never called a "beast". Both are opposed to God, but there's no clear overlap in their actions. The 7 heads and 10 horns might mean that they are the same being, but that's the only real indication.

So the Dragon is clearly Satan. This is explicitly spelled out. It is possible that there is some "dual symbolism" and he is also the Roman Empire, but the case for this is not very strong.

What do the stars represent? Revelation 12:4, speaking of the dragon, says, "His tail drew a third of the stars of heaven and threw them to the earth."

Theory 1: Most commentators say that the stars represent angels who joined Satan in his rebellion against God.

It is frequently said that the Bible often uses stars as symbols for angels. Most notably:

> Revelation 1:20. The mystery of the seven stars which you saw in My right hand, and the seven golden lampstands: The seven stars are the angels of the seven churches, and the seven lampstands which you saw are the seven churches.

But there's a catch. As I noted in section 6.17, the word translated "angels" here may really mean "pastors". I don't know anyone arguing that Revelation 12 means that a third of pastors follow Satan. Though now that I think of it, there are a lot of people out there who call themselves pastors who are not really teaching the Word of God.

Revelation 9:1b. And I saw a star fallen from heaven to the earth. To him was given the key to the bottomless pit.

Without getting into a discussion of what the "bottomless pit" is all about, for our purposes here just note: A "star" falls to Earth, and then "he" is given the key to the bottomless pit. The "star" is treated as a person, "given the key". So many commentators say that the star here is an angel.

But surprisingly – surprising to me, anyway – that's it. I have often read that there are many verses in the Bible that use stars as symbols for angels, or that imply some sort of connection between stars and angels. And so when I started working on this section I wrote that this was so, and then searched for some Bible verses to use as examples. And ... I couldn't find any. I used an electronic Bible and searched every place that the word "star" is used, and couldn't find one that made any connection between stars and angels other than the two debatable connections I just mentioned, Revelation 1 and 9:1.

Side trip: It's common to laugh at the foolishness of other people when they believe things that we know are wrong. Like we laugh at people who believe the world is flat, or that psychics can really tell their future, or at medieval doctors who thought they could cure disease by bleeding the patient. I often wonder what ideas are popular today that people 200 years from now will laugh at as absurd. And I often wonder what things I believe are true because I read it in a book or my parents or a teacher told me it was so or I saw it on TV, that I never examined the evidence for myself. Someone told me, "Science has proven that ..." or "the Bible says that ...", and I just took their word for it without really thinking about it. Well, here's one example. A small one perhaps. But I believed this for years without ever checking.

This certainly doesn't prove that the stars of Revelation 12:4 do *not* represent angels. But it does mean that any such theory must rest on the immediate context and not some general association of stars with angels.

Revelation 12:3 says that the Dragon threw a third of the stars to Earth, and then 12:7 talks about a battle between "Michael and his angels" versus "the dragon and his angels". The fact that the two things are mentioned so close together may mean that they are related, that in fact the stars are angels. Or one could argue that if the stars are angels, why did God switch from using the word "stars" to using the word "angels" so suddenly? If we has going to use the symbol of stars for angels in the beginning of the paragraph, why not continue to use it in the end of the paragraph?

Theory 2: The stars represent nations that have been conquered, either by the Roman Empire or by the Antichrist.

Compare to Daniel 8.

> Daniel 8:8-10. Therefore the male goat grew very great; but when he became strong, the large horn was broken, and in place of it four notable ones came up toward the four winds of heaven. And out of one of them came a little horn which grew exceedingly great toward the south, toward the east, and toward the Glorious *Land.* And it grew up to the host of heaven; and it cast down *some* of the host and *some* of the stars to the ground, and trampled them.

Many of the symbols in this prophecy are explained by the angel Gabriel in verses 15-26. We are told that each animal represents an empire that is to come, and that the goat represents Greece. The prophecy was fulfilled by Alexander the Great.

Note that like the Dragon of Revelation, the goat of Daniel throws stars to the ground. There are a lot of similarities between Daniel and Revelation, so it's plausible to suppose that the stars in Revelation mean the same thing as the stars in Daniel. Which would be very helpful … except that we're not told what the stars in Daniel mean, either.

The most common interpretation is that they represent nations that will be conquered by Greece. Greece under Alexander certainly did conquer many nations, so this is plausible.

Thus, by this theory, the stars that the Dragon casts to the Earth represent conquered nations. Most advocates of this theory say that it means nations conquered by the Roman Empire.

It might also means nations conquered by Satan, that is, nations led into false religions or atheism.

Some commentators connect Daniel 8:24, where Gabriel says that Greece will conquer "the holy people", with verse 10, and say that therefore the stars represent the holy people, which presumably means Israel.

Alexander did indeed conquer Israel, or rather, the Jews practically welcomed him. According to the Jewish historian Jospehus:

> And when he [Alexander the Great] had said this to Parmenion, and had given the high-priest his right hand, the priests ran along by him, and he came into the city. And when he went up into the temple, he offered sacrifice to God, according to the high-priest's direction, and magnificently treated both the high-priest and the priests. And when the Book of Daniel was showed him wherein Daniel declared that one of the Greeks should destroy the empire of the Persians, he supposed that himself was the person intended.
>
> – Josephus, *Antiquities of the Jews*

Alexander was completely correct: Daniel did indeed predict Alexander's conquests, 200 years before the event.

I've never seen a commentator apply this to Revelation, but maybe this means that the Dragon will conquer or destroy a third of Israel or a third of the Jews.

Theory 3: The stars represent Christians who are martyred. When it speaks of Satan sweeping these stars from the sky, it means that he is causing Christians to be killed.

Theory 4: The stars represent Christians turned from the faith by Satan's wiles.

I don't think that theories 3 and 4 are particularly widespread. Neither has any specific scripture to back them up: they're based on trying to interpret from the immediate context.

Another question is the timing of Revelation 12:7-9. When was Satan cast out of Heaven, or is this still in the future?

Most commentators say that this happened very early in the history of the universe, before the creation of human beings or very soon after.

I'm sure we're all familiar with the story in Genesis 3, where Satan tempts Adam and Eve and convinces them to eat the fruit of the Tree of Knowledge, in disobedience of God's command. So Satan must have rebelled against God by then, not long after humans were created, at the very beginning of history. But was he already kicked out of Heaven?

Maybe not.

> Job 1:6-8. Now there was a day when the sons of God came to present themselves before the LORD, and Satan also came among them. And the LORD said to Satan, "From where do you come?" So Satan answered the LORD and said, "From going to and fro on the earth, and from walking back and forth on it." Then the LORD said to Satan, "Have you considered My servant Job, that *there is* none like him on the earth, a blameless and upright man, one who fears God and shuns evil?"

The book of Job tells us that Satan still had access to Heaven by the time of Job. The Bible doesn't tell us clearly when Job lived. It must have been after Noah, because Job 22:16 refers to the Flood in the past tense. Most commentators say Job lived before Moses, because there is no mention in the book of Job about the Ten Commandments or the priesthood, though this is debatable because if Job was not Jewish, these things may have been irrelevant to him. Regardless, let's use around 2100 BC as a working date.

It's possible that Satan was kicked out of Heaven before this, but was still allowed to "visit".

If the events in Revelation 12 are in chronological order,

then Satan is not kicked out of Heaven until after the birth of "the child", who is normally understood to be Jesus.

> Luke 10:17-18. Then the seventy returned with joy, saying, "Lord, even the demons are subject to us in Your name." And He said to them, "I saw Satan fall like lightning from heaven. ..."

So Jesus saw Satan being kicked out of Heaven. As Jesus has existed eternally, this doesn't necessarily mean that Satan was kicked out during Jesus's earthly lifetime. But it does tell us that this event happened before the time when Jesus made this statement, that is, sometime before his crucifixion in AD 34 or so.

Combining the chronology of Revelation 12 with Luke 10, I conclude that Satan was cast out of Heaven sometime during Jesus's earthly lifetime, that is, somewhere between 4 BC and AD 34.

Other commentators say that Revelation 12 is not in chronological order, and so we cannot conclude anything from it about the timing of Satan's expulsion. This is a fair argument. Commentators have long debated whether Revelation as a whole is in chronological order, or whether it is more "topical", a series of scenes each intended to make a point. Many say that sections of Revelation reiterate earlier sections, that John makes a point, and then goes back over the same events to emphasize the point or present additional information. It is not uncommon for writers describing an event to give an overview and then go back and fill in details, or to tell the story from one point of view and then go back to the beginning and tell it from another point of view, etc.

Thus, we end up with three basic theories about the timing of Satan's expulsion:

Theory 1: Before the sin of Adam and Eve. This theory is mostly based on the assumption that Satan would have been kicked out of Heaven immediately upon rebelling against God, and that he clearly had rebelled against God by the time of the Fall.

This requires explaining his presence in Heaven at the time of Job in some way, and assuming that Revelation 12 is not in chronological order.

Theory 2: Sometime during Jesus earthly life, as I explained above. In my opinion, this is the theory that emerges most naturally from the plain reading of all relevant scripture.

Theory 3: At the time of the Second Coming, that is, it is still in the future. This theory is mostly based on the assertion that Revelation is about the Second Coming and that everything in it after chapter 3 is events still in the future. This requires explaining Luke 10 as a prophecy rather than a statement of a past event.

By the way, some commentators say the "the Devil" and "Satan" are two different beings. These verses would seem to pretty clearly say that they are two names for the same being.

6.19. The Beast

Revelation 13:1-8. Then I stood on the sand of the sea. And I saw a beast rising up out of the sea, having seven heads and ten horns, and on his horns ten crowns, and on his heads a blasphemous name. Now the beast which I saw was like a leopard, his feet were like *the feet of* a bear, and his mouth like the mouth of a lion. The dragon gave him his power, his throne, and great authority. And I saw one of his heads as if it had been mortally wounded, and his deadly wound was healed. And all the world marveled and followed the beast. So they worshiped the dragon who gave authority to the beast; and they worshiped the beast, saying, "Who *is* like the beast? Who is able to make war with him?" And he was given a mouth speaking great things and blasphemies, and he was given authority to continue for forty-two months. Then he opened his mouth in blasphemy against God, to blaspheme His name, His tabernacle, and those who dwell in heaven. It was granted to him to make war with the saints and to overcome them. And authority was given him over every tribe, tongue, and nation. All who dwell on the earth will worship him, whose names have not been written in the Book of Life of the Lamb slain from the foundation of the world.

See also, Revelation 17:7-14.

The Beast of Revelation 13 is often compared to the beasts of Daniel 7. Daniel prophesied a series of four empires that would come, beginning in his time. It is not difficult to match each of the empires of Daniel's vision to an empire from history (past to us, future to Daniel):

1. Lion with eagle's wings. Babylon.
2. Bear. Persia.
3. Leopard with four wings and four heads. Greece (Alexander the Great)
4. Creature with 10 horns (not identified as any specific animal). Rome.

But note how the Beast of Revelation incorporates all four of the beasts of Daniel: he has the mouth of a lion, the feet of a bear, generally looks like a leopard, and has ten horns.

Theory 1: The Beast is a future empire, ruled by the Antichrist, that will include the territory of all four of the empires from Daniel. That would mean that it will extend from current-day Spain to parts of India.

Theory 2: The Beast is a future empire that will not necessarily cover this same territory, but that will have characteristics of these empires. It will conquer with the speed of Alexander, have the mechanical determination of Rome, etc. Exactly what that "et cetera" means is debatable: What exactly *are* the defining characteristics of each of these empires?

Theory 3: The beast is the Roman Empire.

One key argument for this theory is Revelation 17:9, "This calls for a mind with wisdom: the seven heads are seven mountains on which the woman is seated". In ancient times, Rome was often called "the city on seven hills". Much like New York City today is called "the Big Apple", Detroit is "Motor

City", Paris is "the city of light", New Orleans is "the Big Easy", and so on. There are other cities in the world with seven hills within their city limits, but few are identified by that fact.

I know of one other city that goes by the nickname, "the city on seven hills": Lisbon, Portugal. I have never heard any Bible commentator link this prophecy in Revelation to Lisbon, Portugal. Probably because Lisbon – and other cities with seven hills -- do not fit the prophecy in other ways. No powerful leader in Lisbon has ever claimed that he was God. Of course, if the fulfillment of the prophecy is still in the future, who knows what will happen. Perhaps centuries from now Lisbon or some other city with seven hills will become the center of such a religion.

Revelation 13:6-8 says that people worship the Beast. The Roman Senate routinely voted to declare the greatest emperors – or at least the least evil and corrupt emperors -- to be gods after their deaths. Personally I find it a little absurd that they thought that they could decide someone was a god by taking a vote in the Senate, but maybe that's no crazier than modern Americans think they can determine the truth about religious and moral issues by taking an opinion poll. Caligula, Nero, and many later emperors didn't want to wait until they died and declared themselves gods while they were still alive, and demanded that people worship them. Some historians see this as a shrewd political move to unite all the diverse people in the empire under one religion that was inextricably tied to the government. Personally I think it was just ego and arrogance, but whatever.

The Roman emperor Nero began the first Roman persecution of Christians after the fire of Rome. According to the historians Suetonius and Tacitus, rumors began to circulate that Nero himself had ordered his henchmen to start the fire. Nero wanted to rebuild the city according to his own master plan, with wide, straight roads; buildings made of stone instead of wood; etc. This may have been his way of removing the existing buildings. Or he may have just done it for fun. Nero was insane: he had his own mother, wife, and son killed.

According to the Roman historian Tacitus:

Therefore, to scotch the rumour, Nero substituted as culprits, and punished with the utmost refinements of cruelty, a class of men, loathed for their vices, whom the crowd styled Christians. Christus, the founder of the name, had undergone the death penalty in the reign of Tiberius, by sentence of the procurator Pontius Pilatus, and the pernicious superstition was checked for a moment, only to break out once more, not merely in Judaea, the home of the disease, but in the capital itself, where all things horrible or shameful in the world collect and find a vogue. First, then, the confessed members of the sect were arrested; next, on their disclosures, vast numbers were convicted, not so much on the count of arson as for hatred of the human race. And derision accompanied their end: they were covered with wild beasts' skins and torn to death by dogs; or they were fastened on crosses, and, when daylight failed were burned to serve as lamps by night. Nero had offered his Gardens for the spectacle, and gave an exhibition in his Circus, mixing with the crowd in the habit of a charioteer, or mounted on his car. Hence, in spite of a guilt which had earned the most exemplary punishment, there arose a sentiment of pity, due to the impression that they were being sacrificed not for the welfare of the state but to the ferocity of a single man.

    – Tacitus. *Annals.* Book XV, paragraph 34.

Revelation 13:7 says that the Beast is given power for 42 months. The fire was in July, AD 64, and the persecution lasted until his death in June, AD 68. That's 47 months, which is tantalizingly close to 42 months. Ancient historians do not say how long it was from the fire until the persecution of Christians began. Could it have been 5 months? Or is the similarity in times just a coincidence?

Revelation 17:14 says that the Beast makes war with the Lamb, but the Lamb overcomes it. The Roman Empire persecuted Christians, but ultimately Christians took over the

Roman Empire.

John tells us that the seven heads also represent seven kings: "Five have fallen, one is, *and* the other has not yet come." (17:9)

Figure 2		
Emperor	**From**	**To**
Julius	ca 49 BC	44 BC
Augustus	27 BC	AD 14
Tiberius	AD 14	AD 37
Caligula	AD 37	AD 41
Claudius	AD 41	AD 54
Nero	AD 54	AD 68
Galba	AD 68	AD 69
Otho	AD 69	AD 69
Vitellius	AD 69	AD 69
Vespasian	AD 69	AD 79
Titus	AD 79	AD 81
Domitian	AD 81	AD 96
Nerva	AD 96	AD 98
Trajan	AD 98	AD 117
Hadrian	AD 117	AD 138

If the beast is Rome, then it would be logical to tie the seven kings to emperors of Rome. But this doesn't seem to work.

Figure 2 lists the Roman emperors who reigned from the beginning of the empire until John's time.

We could debate whether Julius counts as an emperor. It's not like the Romans had a constitutional convention and voted to create this new office of "emperor". The emperors took power by force during a series of civil wars. The English word "emperor" comes from the Latin "IMPERATOR", which was originally an honorary title given to a victorious general by a vote of the soldiers. It didn't come with any political power; it was like being named "man of the year". Julius was acclaimed IMPERATOR in 60 BC and again in 45 BC. Julius did hold the office of "dictator". This was the official name of an office in the Roman republic. A dictator was given broad powers to deal with a crisis, like a war, an epidemic, a corruption scandal, or curiously (to me anyway) to organize sports matches. But his power was not absolute: he was limited to dealing with the crisis he was appointed to solve, he was expected to resign when the crisis was over, and in any case he was limited to six months. For most Roman dictators, it was something of a matter of pride to be able to say, "I have solved the crisis, and so there is no reason for me to continue in this role any longer." But Julius maneuvered to be appointed the first, and only ever, "dictator for life". His efforts to accumulate power led to his assassination, so he never really got to enjoy it. After his death the office of dictator was abolished, but the groundwork was laid for turning an IMPERATOR into what we today think of as a dictator or emperor.

So Julius laid the groundwork for the creation of the position of emperor, but it's debatable if Julius himself was the first emperor or if it was Augustus. The Roman writer Suetonius referred to Julius as the first emperor, but Tacitus started his list with Augustus.

So here's the problem: The book of Revelation was written while John was in prison on the Island of Patmos. Most ancient sources we have say that he was imprisoned there by order of Domitian.

But even if we exclude Julius, Domitian is the 11th emperor, not the 6th. ("Five have fallen, one is …") Some have suggested that Galba, Otho, and Vitellius don't count because their reigns were so short. They all lasted less than a year; the Romans called AD 69 "the year of the four emperors". But that still just brings Domitian down to number 8, not number 6. Even with playing games with the list, it still doesn't work.

At least one ancient source says that John was sent to Patmos by Claudius. Some Preterists then say that he was still there during the reign of Nero. If we count Julius, Nero was the 6th emperor. John says that the 7th king "must remain a little while". The next emperor after Nero was Galba, who reigned only seven months. This could fit the prophecy of "remain a little while".

The catch to this interpretation is that it puts the destruction of Babylon and the Prostitute of Babylon (see section 6.24) during the reign of the 8th Roman emperor, which by this count is Otho. Revelation 19 says that after the fall of Babylon, Christ comes leading an army. Most commentators understand this to be the Second Coming. But if Babylon is Rome, Rome was not destroyed during the reign of Otho, nor did Christ return at that time.

On the other hand, Full Preterists say that references to Christ's return in Revelation do not mean a visible, undeniable return like Futurists suppose. (See section 6.7.) By that theory, the sixth king, the king who "is", is Nero. The seventh king, who will reign only a short time, is Galba. And that takes us just about up to AD 70, when Jerusalem was destroyed by the Romans. Preterists say that this is the fulfillment of the prophecy.

There are some problems with this theory.

One, John tells us that there will be an eighth king, and that the Beast himself is this eighth king. So the eighth king is special, not like the other seven, he is both an eighth king and also an embodiment of the kingdom itself. But the eighth Roman emperor was Otho, who doesn't seem all that special. Arguably, by separating out the eighth king, John is saying that he is not following the regular line here. If we take the eighth king to be Vespasian or Titus, it makes more sense. Before they became emperors, Vespasian and Titus were generals who led the Roman war against Israel. They were the ones most responsible for the destruction of Jerusalem. Vespasian led in the beginning of the war, and Titus was in charge during the siege of Jerusalem. So this sort of works, but it breaks the count.

Two, to make this work you have to pull a fast card trick under the table. The Preterists have to start out by saying that the beast is the Roman Empire and that the seven hills on which the woman sits are the seven hills of Rome. This means that the "Babylon" of Revelation 17 must be Rome. But Rome was not destroyed in AD 70; Jerusalem was. So they have to say that Babylon represents Jerusalem. So the argument begins by saying that the city is Rome, and ends saying that it is Jerusalem.

Theory 4: The Beast is a future, revived Roman Empire.

That is, the old Roman Empire fell in AD 476. But by this theory, the Roman Empire will be rebuilt sometime in the future.

Many Europeans have dreamed of recreating the Roman Empire. Napoleon imagined himself to be the Caesar of a new Roman Empire. Mussolini imagined that he would restore the former greatness of Rome. The rulers of Germany from AD 962 to 1918 were called "Kaiser". In Latin the word "Caesar" is pronounced with the "C" having a "K" sound, that is, the Latin pronunciation is "Kaiser". The Russian title "Tsar" is the Russian equivalent of "Caesar".

When the European Economic Community was established in 1957, many Christians saw this as the first step toward reviving the Roman Empire.

Recall that Revelation says that the Beast has 10 horns. Many Christians took this to mean that the revived Roman Empire would be made up of 10 nations. There were six founding members of the EEC: Italy, Belgium, France, West Germany, Luxembourg, and the Netherlands. In 1973 three more nations joined: Denmark, Ireland, and the United Kingdom. That made 9, which seemed very ominous, just one short of the number needed to fulfill the prophecy. I recall Christians at the time circulating a picture of EEC headquarters with 9 flags flying out front … and one empty flag pole. But then Greece joined in 1981, bringing the number to 10 … and nothing in particular happened. In 1986 Spain and Portugal joined, making 12.

In 1993 the European Union was formed, which absorbed the EEC. The EU now has 28 member countries. (As of this writing, the United Kingdom is in the process of withdrawing.) Clearly more than 10.

Presumably one could argue that the 10 horns do *not* mean 10 countries but something else.

The territory of the European Union overlaps the territory of the old Roman Empire. But, for example, Germany, Poland, and the Baltic states are part of the EU but were never part of the Roman Empire, and Tunisia, Libya, and Egypt were part of the Roman Empire but are not part of the EU. One wouldn't necessarily expect the borders to be identical, but they don't seem very close.

The Roman Empire was, of course, ruled from Rome. Italy and Rome today are part of the EU, but they are not particularly dominant. The headquarters of the EU -- sometimes called the "capital of Europe" -- is in Brussels, Belgium, not in Rome. The EU is mostly dominated by Germany and France, not Italy. On the other hand, the treaty that created the EEC is the "Treaty of Rome", and was negotiated and signed in Rome.

Of course the EU is not presently run by a prophet of a false religion that persecutes Christians. But it is not necessary for the EU to presently meet all the conditions of the prophecy for this to be a viable theory. Charismatic leaders can come to power very quickly. And Europe has been called a "post-Christian society". While the EU is not particularly anti-Christian, it is not pro-Christian either. Only about half of the people in the EU even believe there's a God. Surveys generally show that in western European countries like France and Germany, only 10 to 15% of people who call themselves Christians attend church regularly. So there would be little Christian resistance to someone starting a new religion.

A problem with this theory is that Revelation says that the Beast "was, and is not, and will ascend". At the time that John wrote Revelation, the Roman Empire was near the height of its power. It most certainly did not meet "was, and is not". At the time, one would say "it is". Some try to get around this by saying that John was speaking from the point of view of the time when these prophecies were being fulfilled, not his own time. Someone speaking in 1800 or 1900 could certainly say that the Roman Empire "was, and is not". But by the time of the prophecy, the Beast certainly "is" again. So if John isn't speaking from the point of view of his own time, and isn't speaking from the point of view of the time when the prophecy is fulfilled ... what time is he speaking for?

Most evangelical Christians adhere to this theory.

Theory 5: The Beast represents a series of empires that will rise and fall over the course of history. The seven kings are seven empires.

The exact identification of the seven varies. Most commentators suppose that the seven include the four empires prophesied by Daniel: Babylon, Persia, Greece, and Rome. We expect the prophecies to be consistent with each other. Daniel's prophecy proved accurate: those really were the four great empires following his time. Even without Daniel, people would list these four among the great empires of history. The empire that "now is" in John's time is Rome. So the four empires from Daniel include three that "have fallen" and one that "now is". Revelation says that five have fallen, so we still need two more empires before Rome.

As Daniel was prophesying about empires in his present and future, one obvious possibility is that the other two empires were in Daniel's past. Daniel wouldn't have mentioned past empires in a prophecy about the future. Egypt and Assyria have often been suggested.

That is, the five who have fallen are Egypt, Assyria, Babylon, Persia, and Greece, The one that is now – "now" in John's time – is Rome.

By this reasoning, there would then be one more great empire after Daniel, followed by the special eighth empire, which is the one that supports the Prostitute of Babylon. The British Empire of the 18th and 19th centuries is often given as a candidate for the seventh. Some suggest the "American Empire" of the 20th century. There's a bit of a problem here that, if we are following a Futurist interpretation that all of this is still in the future, there are too many candidates. There have been a number of empires comparable in power to Babylon, Greece, and Rome: in the West, there is Spain, France, Britain, maybe America. In Asia there is the Mongols, the Qing in China, and Russia. In the Middle East there are the successive Muslim caliphates, and the Ottomans. If John is looking forward to all of history from his own time until the second coming, why does he say just two more great empires and not a dozen or more? We have to conclude either that most of the empires of history "don't count" for some reason, or that the prophecy is not for the future, that at least this portion was fulfilled in the past. Our past, that is; John's future.

The Preterist theory that all this was fulfilled in the destruction of Jerusalem doesn't help here. It gives the opposite problem: too few kings/empires. If the five past kings are Egypt, Assyria, Babylon, Persia, and Greece, and the present king is Rome, then Jerusalem was destroyed during the time of the sixth king. There was no number seven or eight in between.

Theory 6: The Beast is an Islamic Caliphate. That is, the Beast is a Muslim empire that will be formed sometime in the future from many Muslim nations.

After the death of Muhammad, his empire broke up into many separate nations. Today there are 57 Muslim nations in the world. Muslims are divided into Sunni and Shia sects, somewhat like Christians are divided into Protestants and Catholics, and Sunnis and Shiites often fight each other. (Whenever Sunnis are in power, they tend to persecute Shiites, and whenever Shiites are in power, they persecute Sunnis. The only country in the Middle East where both Sunnis and Shiites have full legal rights is … Israel.)

Three of Daniel's four empires are now ruled by Muslims. The Bear, Persia, become Muslim in AD 642; the Lion, Babylon, in 651, and most of the Leopard, Alexander's empire, in 1458. The original base of Alexander's empire, Macedonia and Greece, rebelled and gained its independence in 1821. So Greece and Macedonia are now Christian/secular, but the rest is Muslim.

Muhammad could certainly be described as an anti-Christ. He acknowledged that Jesus lived, and indeed that he was born to a virgin:

> The angels said to Mary: "Allah bids you rejoice in
> a Word from Him. His name is the Messiah, Jesus the son
> of Mary. He shall be noble in this world and in the next,

and he shall be favoured by Allah. He shall preach to men in his cradle and in the prime of his manhood, and shall lead a righteous life." "Lord," she said, "how can I bear a child when no man has touched me?" He replied, "Such is the will of Allah. He creates whom He will. When He decrees a thing He need only say: "Be," and it is.

— Quran 3:45-38.

But Muhammad denied that Jesus was God made flesh. Muslims say that Jesus was a prophet, but nothing more.

People of the Book, do not transgress the bounds of your religion. Speak nothing but the truth about Allah. The Messiah, Jesus the son of Mary, was no more than Allah's apostle and His Word which He cast to Mary: a spirit from Him. So believe in Allah and His apostles and do not say: "Three". Forbear, and it shall be better for you. Allah is but one God. Allah forbid that He should have a son!

— Quran 4:171

Muslims say that Jesus was a great prophet, but not as great as Muhammad. They deny that he rose from the dead. According to Islam, Jesus ascended into Heaven without ever dying, like Elijah.

The Bible says that the Antichrist is someone who denies that Jesus is the son of God.

1 John 2:22-23. Who is a liar but he who denies that Jesus is the Christ? He is antichrist who denies the Father and the Son. Whoever denies the Son does not have the Father either; he who acknowledges the Son has the Father also.

So Muhammad and Islam clearly fit.

There have been numerous efforts to unite Muslims under a single ruler. Traditionally a Muslim ruler is called a "caliph", so this goal is often called the Caliphate.

The first caliphate was the Rashidun Caliphate, AD 632 to 661. The most recent was the Ottoman Empire. They declared themselves a caliphate in 1517, and survived until they were among the losers in World War 1 and the empire was dismantled. At their peak in the late 1600s, they ruled Turkey, the Middle East, Egypt, the northern coast of Africa, Greece and the Balkans.

In 2014, ISIS declared that it was creating a new caliphate. As of this writing (2018) ISIS appears to be just about destroyed, so barring some dramatic resurgence, they are not going to succeed

While there are many political and religious divisions among Muslims, it is not hard to imagine a charismatic leader managing to unite a number of Muslim nations under himself and then taking over the rest by some combination of persuasion, force, and intimidation.

In recent years there has been a large influx of Muslims into western Europe. About 5% of western Europe is now Muslim, over 8% in France and Sweden. Not a huge percentage, but if Islam keeps growing and Christianity keeps shrinking, Europe could soon be more Muslim and Christian.

When discussing Theory 1 I said that some say there will be a future empire that includes all or most of the territory controlled by the four empires of Daniel combined. When Islam was at its peak during the Umayyad Caliphate, AD 661-750, Islam controlled lands from Spain to India. They didn't control all the territory that had been part of the Roman Empire. They didn't have Italy, Gaul, Greece and some other lands in Europe. But they controlled about half of the old Roman Empire: Spain, north Africa, and the Middle East. If at some point in the future Muslims did manage to take over some large section of Europe, they could fit the prophecy quite well. Is that likely to happen? Not tomorrow, but, etc.

Theory 7: In a different direction, some commentators say that the Beast is not an empire, but a person. They connect him with the Antichrist (section 6.20), the Man of Lawlessness (section 6.21), and the Prince Who is to Come (section 6.22). But note that nowhere does scripture explicitly connect any of these people. They have similarities, so they *might* be the same person, but that is an interpretation and not an explicit teaching of scripture.

Most of the description of the Beast could refer to a man or to an empire. He has authority and power. A man can have power, or an empire can have power. People worship the Beast. Again, that could be a man or an empire.

But a few things make it sound like a man.

Revelation 13:5 says, "And he was given a mouth speaking great things and blasphemies". That sounds more like a person than an empire.

13:12 says that the False Prophet (section 6.25) "exercises all the authority of the first beast in his presence". You can be in the presence of a man. It's hard to see how you can be in the presence of an empire. 13:14 says that the False Prophet "make[s] an image of the Beast". Again, you can make an image of a man. Not so clear how you make an image of an empire. 13:18 says that the number of the Beast is "the number of a man".

On the other hand, the Beast is a symbol. Whether the Beast is a man or an empire, in the prophecy he is represented by a strange creature. So when the prophecy sounds like it's talking about an individual, it could be talking about the creature that John is shown that represents an empire, rather than talking about an actual person.

This theory is often tied to one of the other theories, saying that the Beast is the ruler of one of the empires described by the other theories

A specific identification that was popular in the early days of Christianity was that the Beast was the Roman Emperor Nero. In John's time there were rumors that Nero had escaped the assassination and was still alive, and that he would come back to reclaim the throne. As the years went by these rumors turned into legends, at times making Nero an almost messianic figure with his own "second coming". Some Christians tied this to the part of the prophecy that the beast "was, is not, and is to come". I think you would be hard-pressed to find people who advocate this particular version of the theory today. Nero is clearly long dead, and I don't know of anyone who believes that Nero is coming back from the dead.

One statement about the Beast that has attracted attention on its own is Revelation 13:3. "And I saw one of his heads as if it had been mortally wounded, and his deadly wound was healed. And all the world marveled and followed the beast." What does it mean when it says that the Beast has a wound that was healed?

Theory 1: Those who believe the Beast is an empire and that the heads represent nations making up this empire interpret this to mean that one nation was destroyed, but was then revived, or that one nation broke away from the empire, but was then brought back in.

I haven't read any commentator suggesting this, but just a personal musing based on contemporary politics: If the Beast is a revived Roman Empire and that empire is the European Union, then, as I write this, the United Kingdom is in the process of breaking away. If the EU politicians manage to stop this process, or if the UK leaves and later comes back, perhaps that would be a fulfillment of the prophecy. But whether the nation that leaves and comes back is Britain or someone else, why is this a "big deal" worth mentioning in the prophecy? It seems like a minor detail, and we're not told any reason why it is important.

Theory 2: Those who believe that the Beast is a person rather than an empire say this is literal: This person receives some deadly wound, and then the wound is miraculously healed. Usually they suppose literally miraculously. This leads people to follow the Beast because they think he has divine powers or at least psychic powers.

Some early Christians said that the Roman emperor Caligula fit the prophecy. A few months after becoming emperor in AD 37, Caligula became extremely sick and it was thought he would die. But then he recovered, seemingly miraculously. So some tied this to the prophecy and said that Caligula was the Beast.

A problem with this is that Caligula did not have a "wound", he had an illness. He may have been poisoned. Revelation says he was "wounded by the sword". Also, Caligula doesn't seem to fit the prophecy in other ways.

6.20. Antichrist

There are three places in the Bible that use the word "Antichrist". Interestingly, none of them are in Revelation: they are in 1 and 2 John.

> 1 John 2:18-19, 22. Little children, it is the last hour; and as you have heard that the Antichrist is coming, even now many antichrists have come, by which we know that it is the last hour. They went out from us, but they were not of us; for if they had been of us, they would have continued with us; but *they went out* that they might be made manifest, that none of them were of us. ... Who is a liar but he who denies that Jesus is the Christ? He is antichrist who denies the Father and the Son.

> 1 John 4:2-3. By this you know the Spirit of God: Every spirit that confesses that Jesus Christ has come in the flesh is of God, and every spirit that does not confess that Jesus Christ has come in the flesh is not of God. And this is the *spirit* of the Antichrist, which you have heard was coming, and is now already in the world.

> 2 John 1:7. For many deceivers have gone out into the world who do not confess Jesus Christ *as* coming in the flesh. This is a deceiver and an antichrist.

Many commentators connect the Antichrist to the Beast of Revelation.

The Bible does not make any explicit connection between the two. The idea that the Beast is the Antichrist is not based on any specific Biblical statement, but rather is conjecture based on similarities in the description.

Indeed, John here clearly says that "antichrist" is not one

specific person, but a type of person: one who denies that Jesus is the Christ, i.e. the Messiah. He says that there are "many antichrists".

Furthermore, John says that "even now many antichrists have come", and "the spirit of the Antichrist … is now already in the world". It is difficult to see how to read this other than to say that at the time the epistles of John were written, antichrists were already in the world. John's epistles were written about AD 90, probably a few years before he wrote Revelation.

In my opinion, I have difficulty seeing a connection between the antichrists and the Beast. Especially when you consider that the epistles of John and Revelation were written by the same person, within a few years of each other. If he wanted to say that he was talking about the same person, why didn't he use the same word?

Perhaps you could say that John means that there is one "ultimate Antichrist" who will come at some time in the future, but that there will be many "little antichrists" in the meantime.

6.21. Man of Lawlessness

2 Thessalonians 2:1-10. Now, brethren, concerning the coming of our Lord Jesus Christ and our gathering together to Him, we ask you, not to be soon shaken in mind or troubled, either by spirit or by word or by letter, as if from us, as though the day of Christ had come. Let no one deceive you by any means; for *that Day will not come* unless the falling away comes first, and the man of sin is revealed, the son of perdition, who opposes and exalts himself above all that is called God or that is worshiped, so that he sits as God in the temple of God, showing himself that he is God. Do you not remember that when I was still with you I told you these things? And now you know what is restraining, that he may be revealed in his own time. For the mystery of lawlessness is already at work; only He who now restrains *will do so* until He is taken out of the way. And then the lawless one will be revealed, whom the Lord will consume with the breath of His mouth and destroy with the brightness of His coming. The coming of the *lawless one* is according to the working of Satan, with all power, signs, and lying

wonders, and with all unrighteous deception among those who perish, because they did not receive the love of the truth, that they might be saved.

The New King James that I quote above calls this person the "man of sin". The Revised Standard Version and many other English translations translate this as the "man of lawlessness", and I think that's the more common term for him.

Apparently some of the Thessalonians thought that the Second Coming had already happened. But Paul says here that before the Second Coming, the "man of lawlessness" must be revealed, and that Christ will then defeat him.

As the Man of Lawlessness apparently comes shortly before the Second Coming, it is not a stretch to try to connect him to events in Revelation.

Many commentators connect him to the Beast (section 6.19) and/or to the Antichrist (section 6.20).

He does seem to match some of what his said about the Beast:

1. Both arrive on the scene shortly before the Second Coming.

2. Both are worshipped as God.

3. God destroys them both.

Also, the Man of Lawlessness "sits in the temple of God" claiming to be God. This sounds like the Abomination of Desolation (section 6.2). If the Man of Lawlessness is the Beast, then this ties together Daniel, Matthew, and Revelation.

6.22. Prince Who Is To Come

At the end of Daniel's prophecy of the 70 weeks (section 6.3), the prophet talks about a "prince who is to come":

Daniel 9:26-27. And after the sixty-two weeks, an anointed one shall be cut off, and shall have nothing; and the people of the prince who is to come shall destroy the city and the sanctuary. Its end shall come with a flood, and to the end there shall be war; desolations are decreed. And he shall make a strong covenant with many for one week; and for half of the week he shall cause sacrifice and offering to cease; and upon the wing of abominations shall come one who makes desolate, until the decreed end is poured out on the desolator.

Theory 1: The most common Futurist theory is that the prince is the Beast of Revelation (section 6.19). He arrives on the scene shortly before the Second Coming, some time in the future.

As the sanctuary was in Jerusalem, "the city and the sanctuary" presumably means Jerusalem.

Note that Daniel does not say that "the prince" destroys Jerusalem, but rather that "the people of the prince" destroy Jerusalem. By this theory, this means that the Prince comes long after the destruction of Jerusalem, but that he comes from the same nation as the people who destroy Jerusalem.

Jerusalem was destroyed by the Romans in AD 70. As "the people" would be the Romans, then the "prince who is to come" must be an Italian. That is, the Beast will be Italian. Or some say more generally, a European.

An alternate theory is that the Prince will be an Arab. According to the Roman historian Tacitus:

> Early in this same year [AD 70] Titus Caesar had been entrusted by his father with the task of completing the reduction of Judaea. ... Three legions awaited him in Judaea, the Fifth, Tenth, and Fifteenth, all veterans from his father's army. These were reinforced by the Twelfth from Syria and by detachments of the Twenty-second and the Third, brought over from Alexandria. This force was accompanied by twenty auxiliary cohorts and eight regiments of auxiliary cavalry besides the Kings Agrippa and Sohaemus, King Antiochus' irregulars, a strong force of Arabs, who had a neighbourly hatred for the Jews ...

– Tacitus, *The Histories*, Book 5.

Some point out that of the six legions that Titus had when he attacked Jerusalem, three were from Syria and two from Egypt. Only one was from Europe. But we should take this with caution. Just because a legion was stationed in Syria or Egypt doesn't mean that the soldiers came from Syria or Egypt. Just because a United States military unit is stationed in Afghanistan doesn't mean that the soldiers are Afghans. Only Roman citizens were eligible to be members of a legion. For example, the Third Legion – one of the legions that Tacitus lists as being part of the attack -- was originally raised in Italy, fought in Gaul (France) and the civil wars in Italy, and then much later was sent to Egypt to put down anti-Roman revolts. Non-Romans served as "auxiliaries". I should note that people outside Italy were often given Roman citizenship, which gave important legal privileges. The apostle Paul, although Jewish and born in Tarsus, which is in modern Turkey, was legally a Roman citizen, Acts 22:22-29. Sometimes entire towns were given Roman citizenship as a reward for some service to the empire.

In any case, the auxiliaries mentioned were certainly non-Romans. The Roman army was joined by many soldiers from other Middle Eastern countries who hated the Jews and were happy to join in an attack on them. The Jewish historian Josephus also says that most of the soldiers were Arabs or other Middle Eastern people.

So although the army attacking Jerusalem was led by a Roman and fought under the banner of Rome, many or most of the soldiers in the army were Arabs. Arguably, then, "the people of the prince who is to come" means Arabs and not Romans.

Note that they would not have been Muslims, as the religion of Islam would not exist until about AD 610, 540 years after the destruction of Jerusalem.

Daniel's "weeks" are usually interpreted to mean periods of 7 years – see section 6.3. So this Prince comes at the end of history and makes a treaty with many nations, including Israel, for 7 years. Empowered by this treaty, Israel rebuilds the temple and resumes the Old Testament sacrifices. But then halfway through the 7 years he betrays Israel and stops the sacrifices. Then at the end of the 7 years, Christ returns and destroys him.

Theory 2: The Preterist theory is that all of this happens at the time of the destruction of Jerusalem in AD 70. The distinction between "the prince" and "the people of the prince" is simply that one man cannot destroy a city alone. He must lead an army to destroy Jerusalem, so it talks about "the people". But one man can sign a treaty, so when it talks about the treaty it is just "he". The covenant he makes is not with Israel, but with people who joined with the Romans to attack Jerusalem, most notably the Arabs. But ultimately he will be judged by God.

Theory 3: A very different theory is that the Prince is Christ. Daniel 9:25 speaks of "Messiah the Prince", then 9:26 again mentions "Messiah", and then in the next sentence, "the prince who is to come". As the word "prince" is used twice in two verses, it makes sense to suppose that it's referring to the same person both times. As the first reference is clearly to the Messiah, then both references must be to the Messiah.

Then the "people of the prince" are the Jews. Of course the Jews did not destroy Jerusalem themselves in AD 70, but advocates of this view say that they brought the destruction on themselves, perhaps in a political sense by foolishly starting a war with Rome, or in a practical sense by fighting amongst themselves while the city was under siege (see section 6.4), or in a spiritual sense by rejecting the Messiah.

Alternatively, "the people" could mean "people sent by the Messiah". Jesus used the Romans as his instrument to punish Jerusalem, just as God used the Assyrians and Babylonians as his instrument to punish Israel hundreds of years before.

Christ caused the sacrifices to end because they were no longer necessary after he became the perfect sacrifice. The "desolator" is not the same person as the prince.

6.23. Woman with the child

Revelation 12:1-6. Now a great sign appeared in heaven: a woman clothed with the sun, with the moon under her feet, and on her head a garland of twelve stars. Then being with child, she cried out in labor and in pain to give birth. And another sign appeared in heaven: behold, a great, fiery red dragon having seven heads and ten horns, and seven diadems on his heads. His tail drew a third of the stars of heaven and threw them to the earth. And the dragon stood before the woman who was ready to give birth, to devour her Child as soon as it was born. She bore a male Child who was to rule all nations with a rod of iron. And her Child was caught up to God and His throne. Then the woman fled into the wilderness, where she has a place prepared by God, that they should feed her there one thousand two hundred and sixty days.

Revelation 12:13-17. Now when the dragon saw that he had been cast to the earth, he persecuted the woman who gave birth to the male *Child*. But the woman was given two wings of a great eagle, that she might fly into the wilderness to her place, where she is nourished for a time and times and half a time, from the presence of the serpent. So the serpent spewed water out of his mouth like a flood after the woman, that he might cause her to be carried away by the flood. But the earth helped the woman, and the earth opened its mouth and swallowed up the flood which the dragon had spewed out of his mouth. And the dragon was enraged with the woman, and he went to make war with the rest of her offspring, who keep the commandments of God and have the testimony of Jesus Christ.

Note that we are told these are "signs", not necessarily literal events.

Almost all commentators agree that the child is Jesus. Revelation 19:15 says that Christ will rule with a rod of iron, just like the child here. Satan did try to kill Jesus as soon as he was born. And Jesus did ascend to Heaven.

So who is the woman?

Theory 1: The Church. By this theory, the 12 stars over the woman's head are the 12 apostles.

Verse 17 fits this theory well: If Jesus was the Church's child, then "the rest of her offspring" would be all Christians. And Satan has certainly made war with the Church and

Christians.

A problem with this theory is that it turns the metaphor on its head: The Church did not give birth to Christ; Christ gave birth to the Church.

Theory 2: Israel. The 12 stars are the 12 tribes. As Jesus was born a Jew, he was a child of Israel. This is probably the most common theory among Christians.

It does make verse 17 awkward. "The rest of her offspring" would then presumably mean Jews in general. Satan certainly has persecuted the Jews. But Jews do not all "have the testimony of Jesus Christ". Many commentators say that verse 17 is referring to Jewish Christians and not Jews in general.

Theory 3: Mary. Mary was literally the mother of Jesus. This is mostly a Catholic theory.

Theory 4: Mary Baker Eddy, founder of the Christian Science church. This is, of course a Christian Science theory, not taken very seriously by anyone else.

Mary Baker Eddy did not give birth to Christ. Christian Scientists call her "Mother" and consider her the spiritual mother of all their members, so the reference to "the rest of her offspring" could presumably mean all Christian Scientists.

One might expect that we could use the other information given here about the woman to narrow down her identity. But unfortunately, the meaning of the rest of the story is also debated.

We are told that the woman fled into the wilderness where she was protected by God for 1260 days. Satan tries to attack her with a flood, but the earth swallows the water and she is safe. Then in frustration Satan attacks her other children.

Are the 1260 days literal days? That would be about 3 ½ years. Some Preterists say this refers to the Jews final defense against Rome at Masada, a fortress in the desert. But the text indicates that the attack on the woman in her wilderness hide-out failed, while historically the Romans ultimately conquered

Masada. It took a long siege and a bloody battle, but the Jews lost in the end. Nevertheless, if this is the correct interpretation, then the woman is the Jews.

Futurists say that this refers to a future time. The Antichrist will attack Israel, and the Jews will retreat to some fortress in the wilderness where they will hold out for 3 ½ years, at which time Christ will return to end the siege. Again, this would mean that the woman is the Jews.

One could theorize that this is a prophecy of a future time when Christians will retreat into the wilderness, but I don't know anyone who says that.

Some commentators say that this doesn't fit Jesus's literal mother Mary, because she never hid in the wilderness for 3 ½ years. But Joseph and Mary did flee to Egypt. We know very little about this trip. We don't know if they lived in the wilderness in Egypt or in a major city. We don't know how long they stayed there.

Most historians conclude Jesus was born somewhere between 6 BC and 4 BC. Matthew tells us:

> Matthew 6:19-20. Now when Herod was dead, behold, an angel of the Lord appeared in a dream to Joseph in Egypt, saying, "Arise, take the young Child and His mother, and go to the land of Israel, for those who sought the young Child's life are dead."

This implies they returned to Israel shortly after the death of Herod. This was in 4 BC, which would seem to have them in Egypt for perhaps two years, maybe as little as a few months. On the other hand, it's possible that God did not tell them to return *immediately* upon the death of Herod, or that the command to return was not particularly urgent. Nothing in the Bible or history rules out the possibility that they stayed in Egypt for several years. So 3 ½ years is possible.

Other commentators say that when prophecy says a "day", here and elsewhere, it means a year. So 1260 days would mean 1260 years. I have always had a problem with this interpretation: Why would God say "day" when he means "year"? Until someone shows me a prophecy that was clearly fulfilled if we interpret "day" to mean "year", I'm going to doubt this. But even if we accept it here, there is no obvious period of history when either Israel or the Church took refuge in the wilderness for 1260 years. The most straightforward reading of the text has the flight to the wilderness happening shortly after Jesus is caught up to Heaven. So by this theory we'd have to say that God protected Israel or the Church in some way beginning AD 34 or not long after and continuing for about 1260 years, so up to AD 1294 or so. There are no apparent historical events that fulfill such an interpretation of prophecy.

It's possible that it is referring to Israel's "wilderness wandering" following the Exodus. God did carry Israel to safety from the Egyptians to the wilderness. Perhaps the flood from Satan's mouth means the power of Egypt to keep the Israelis in slavery, or perhaps it means the flood of words to lead Israel astray, leading up to the golden calf, the grumbling about the manna, Korah's rebellion, etc. (I haven't seen the part about the flood in any commentary: that's a theory I just made up.) But the rest of the description doesn't really fit. Revelation seems to say that this flight to the wilderness happens after the birth of Christ, while of course the Exodus was long before. It says it lasts for 1260 days, while the wilderness wanderings lasted for 40 years.

By this theory, this passage is not a prophecy, of course, because it's long past, but rather showing how the history of Israel fits into the prophecy.

Perhaps "wilderness" here is a symbol that stands for something else. By most theories the woman is not a literal woman and the water from the dragon's mouth is not literal water from a literal dragon's mouth. But at that point there are so many symbols for which we have no clear interpretation that we don't know where to start. Some unidentified person or group symbolized by the woman will take refuge in some unidentified place or situation symbolized by the wilderness where she will be attacked in some unidentified manner symbolized by water and defended in some unidentified way by something symbolized by the earth. And this will happen over a period of 1260 unidentified units of time.

Some commentators try to identify the symbols. Many say that the waters from the dragon's mouth represent nations, and point to Revelation 17:5, speaking of another symbolic woman, "The waters which you saw, where the harlot sits, are peoples, multitudes, nations, and tongues." So, they say, "water" represents nations. Thus this verse means that Satan sends many nations to attack Israel.

But also in Revelation, several places use "water" to describe the sound made by the voice of God or of a mighty angel. See 1:15, 14:2, 19:6. Rev 7:17 talks of Christ leading people to "fountains of living water", probably alluding to John 4:10 and John 7:48 where Jesus described himself as "living water". Rev 16:4 talks about "rivers and springs of water", probably literal water. Etc. So water does not symbolize nations throughout Revelation. We only have one place where this symbolism is clearly stated and a dozen or so where it is unlikely or impossible.

The flood from the dragon's mouth *might* mean that Satan sends many nations to attack Israel. Or it might mean that he sends a literal flood. Or it might mean something else.

What are the "wings of a great eagle" that carry the woman to the place of safety?

Some say this means that Israel (or the Church) is carried to safety by aircraft. Some commentators say that the reference to an eagle means that the airlift is provided by the United States, because of course the eagle is the symbol of the United States.

But many countries use the eagle as a national symbol. The flags of Albania, Egypt, Kazakhstan, Mexico, Moldova, Montenegro, Serbia, and Zambia all picture eagles. (And Zimbabwe's flag shows an image of a bird that is found in ancient sculptures and which may be an eagle, but no one knows for sure.) The coats of arms of Armenia, Germany, Indonesia,

Mexico, Namibia, Panama, Poland, Russia, and South Sudan include eagles.

If the eagle represents a country, it could be any of these. This isn't necessarily a complete list: it's just ones I knew, or could find in a quick web search.

In Exodus, God says to Moses:

> Exodus 19:4. You have seen what I did to the Egyptians, and *how* I bore you on eagles' wings and brought you to Myself.

Clearly when the Israelis left Egypt, they did not travel by airplane, nor did they literally fly in any other way. God uses the phrase "on eagles' wings" here as a poetic way to describe their escape, probably referring to the speed or the way they were able to pass over barriers.

The similarity of the wording between Exodus and Revelation may be significant. This is an argument in favor of saying that Revelation 12 is talking about the Exodus. Or it may mean that Israel will be taken to a place of safety in the same way that God took Israel to safety during the Exodus. God did it once before; he will do it again.

All told, it is difficult to match Revelation 12 to any past event, before or after Revelation was written. This may mean that it is not yet fulfilled. Or it may mean that we don't understand it.

6.24. Prostitute of Babylon

Revelation talks about a woman it calls the Prostitute of Babylon.

Some, mostly older, translations call her the Whore of Babylon or the Harlot of Babylon. Personally I find the words "whore" and "harlot" a little crude and I avoid using them, so I'll stick with "prostitute" here. (Because "prostitute" is such a positive, uplifting word!)

The section about her in Revelation is rather long so I won't quote the whole thing here. I encourage you to read Revelation 16:17 through the end of Revelation 18. But to excerpt:

> Revelation 17:1b-6a. "Come, I will show you the judgment of the great harlot who sits on many waters, with whom the kings of the earth committed fornication, and the inhabitants of the earth were made drunk with the wine of her fornication." So he carried me away in the Spirit into the wilderness. And I saw a woman sitting on a scarlet beast *which was* full of names of blasphemy, having seven heads and ten horns. The woman was arrayed in purple and scarlet, and adorned with gold and precious stones and pearls, having in her hand a golden cup full of abominations and the filthiness of her fornication. And on her forehead a name *was* written: MYSTERY, BABYLON THE GREAT, THE MOTHER OF HARLOTS AND OF THE ABOMINATIONS OF THE EARTH. I saw the woman, drunk with the blood of the saints and with the blood of the martyrs of Jesus.

What does this woman represent?

Throughout the Bible, prostitution is often used as a symbol for false religion. For example:

> Leviticus 20:5-6. Then I will set My face against that man and against his family; and I will cut him off from his people, and all who prostitute themselves with him to commit harlotry with Molech. And the person who turns to mediums and familiar spirits, to prostitute himself with them, I will set My face against that person and cut him off from his people.

> Exodus 34:14-15a. (for you shall worship no other god, for the LORD, whose name *is* Jealous, *is* a jealous God), lest you make a covenant with the inhabitants of the land, and they play the harlot with their gods ...

God is making an analogy between false religions and prostitution. People were created to worship God. In particular, Jews, and now Christians, have a special loving relationship with God. He is our God and we are his people. It's like a marriage. Indeed, Revelation refers to the Church as the bride of Christ – Revelation 21:2 and 9. So if Jehovah is our "husband" and we then chase after some other god, that's comparable to adultery.

So almost all commentators agree that the Prostitute of

Babylon is a false religion.

At the time Revelation was written, the city of Babylon had been abandoned. Alexander the Great conquered Babylon in 331 BC and made it practically the "eastern capital" of his empire. The city boomed. But when Alexander died in 323 BC, it was torn apart by civil strife, and the remaining inhabitants were exiled in 275 BC. (See section 6.15.) While it was not totally destroyed – it was not burned to the ground or demolished – it was a ghost town. So when John wrote about Babylon as a great and prosperous city in Revelation, he was not thinking of the Babylon of his own day. Babylon was further past to John than the American Revolution is to us.

So tied up with the question of identifying the prostitute is identifying "Babylon". There are five basic theories here.

Theory 1: The literal city of Babylon. At some time in the future, Babylon will be rebuilt and will become the center of an influential false religion.

While Babylon is basically abandoned today, Arabs periodically talk about rebuilding it. Babylon is within the borders of modern Iraq. Sadam Hussein started a project to rebuild Babylon in the 1980s, but it was aborted by the Gulf War. It's possible that some future Arab leader will succeed in rebuilding Babylon. If this was to happen in the near future, the city would likely quickly become a center for Islam.

Some commentators reject this theory because of a prophecy in Isaiah saying that Babylon would never be rebuilt:

> Isaiah 13:19-20. And Babylon, the glory of kingdoms, The beauty of the Chaldeans' pride, Will be as when God overthrew Sodom and Gomorrah. It will never be inhabited, Nor will it be settled from generation to generation; Nor will the Arabian pitch tents there, Nor will the shepherds make their sheepfolds there.

Others say that this prophecy is not yet fulfilled. They say that Babylon was never destroyed in the way described in the prophecy, and so this must be talking about some future destruction. Most who take this position then link it to the prophecy we are discussing in Revelation, saying that Isaiah 13 and Revelation 17 and 18 are describing the same event. If that's true, then Isaiah's statement that Babylon will never again be inhabited would mean that it would never again be inhabited after this future destruction.

Theory 2: "Babylon" is used as a symbol or metaphor for corrupt religion.

It's common enough for a place to also symbolize some broader human activity. If I say "Hollywood" you might think of the literal city in California. But you also might think of the movie industry. Madison Avenue is a literal street in New York City, but it is also often used to refer to advertising. Sodom was a literal city in the Middle East, but it is also a symbol for sin, especially homosexuality. The Rubicon is a literal river in Italy, but it is also a symbol for a fateful decision. Etc. Revelation may be using the word "Babylon" as a symbol for the sort of pagan religion that flourished in Babylon.

Theory 3: John uses the name "Babylon" as a sort of code word for Rome. He could not just say "Rome" because then the Romans would have prevented distribution of the book of Revelation.

If John had written that Rome was a corrupt city and that God was going to destroy it, the Romans might have tried to prevent his book from being published. Rome certainly had the political power to make it difficult for him. He was in a Roman prison colony when he wrote it so they might simply have never let his manuscript leave the prison.

Some commentators say that there is a precedent for this: They say that 1 Peter 3:13 uses "Babylon" as a code word for Rome. At the end of his letter Peter passes on greetings from various other people:

1 Peter 3:12-13. By Silvanus, our faithful brother as I consider him, I have written to you briefly, exhorting and testifying that this is

the true grace of God in which you stand. She who is in Babylon, elect together with *you*, greets you; and *so does* Mark my son.

Peter may have been in Rome when he wrote this letter, and so he may have been passing on greetings from the church at Rome.

But there's nothing in 1 Peter to indicate that "Babylon" here is a code word, and we don't actually know where Peter was when he wrote this letter. There's no clear reason for Peter to hide the name of the city in his letter. The Romans knew that there were Christians in Rome, and Peter isn't saying anything nasty about Babylon/Rome here.

Many say that "she" refers to a church and not an individual woman, though again it's not clear why Peter would be obscure about this. If he meant a church, why didn't he say "the church at ..." On the other hand, if he meant a literal woman, why didn't he say her name like he said "Silvanus" and "Mark" rather than a vague "she".

Peter was certainly in Rome during his lifetime, and so he could have known a woman or a church from that city. Advocates of this theory point out that Peter was probably never in the literal city of Babylon. But even if he was never there, he might have known someone that he met elsewhere and who then travelled to Babylon. I know people who have travelled to places that I have never been.

Some suggest that Peter is referring to a city named Babylon that was in Egypt. There was a small city called Babylon in Egypt, probably named after the original Babylon. Just like there is a Bethlehem in Israel and also a Bethlehem in the US state of Pennsylvania. The reference to Babylon comes just before a mention of Mark, and Mark spent considerable time in Egypt, so maybe there's a connection.

So all told, I conclude that Peter is of little help in understanding the reference to Babylon in Revelation. You can't take a debatable theory that you have spun about one difficult Bible verse and use it to prove something about another difficult Bible verse.

A response to the idea that Babylon here is Rome and John was being obscure to avoid the Romans blocking publication is that an all-powerful God could not have been stopped by such human efforts. But God generally works through human agencies. Maybe the way God chose to prevent such human interference was by using such a "code name" in the book.

Theory 4: Similar to theory 3, except that instead of Babylon being a code word for Rome, some say that it was a code word for Jerusalem. In this case, by the time the book of Revelation was written Israel had been destroyed and the Jews had virtually no political power, so it is unlikely that John would have tried to confuse identification of the city for political reasons. The more likely reason is that he is trying to make a point, that he is saying that Jerusalem had become as corrupt and evil as ancient Babylon.

Theory 5: Some future city that did not exist at the time Revelation was written. This city will be like Babylon in some ways, and so for convenience John calls it Babylon.

One might say, But why wouldn't God have just told John what the name of the city will be? If God in his foreknowledge knows what the city will be like, what it will do, and how it will be destroyed, doesn't he know its name? But perhaps giving the name would have interfered with the operation of the prophecy. If God said that this evil, doomed city will be called, whatever, say "Fwacbar", then no Christian would ever name a city "Fwacbar".

The woman is riding on a beast, and the identification of the woman is thus intertwined with the identification of the Beast. (See section 6.19.)

To look at these theories another way: To the Preterist, looking for a past fulfillment of this prophecy, there are three fairly obvious candidates for an evil city that made war against the Christian Church:

Option 1. Jerusalem. The Jewish leaders arranged to have Jesus crucified and they persecuted Christians.

Option 2. Ancient Rome. The Roman Empire persecuted Christians from the time of Nero until Constantine.

Option 3. Medieval Rome. The Catholic Church became corrupt and fought against Protestants and reformers for centuries.

The theory that Babylon is the Roman Catholic Church was very popular among Protestants from the Reformation to at least the early 20th century. As relations between Catholics and Protestants have improved, it is, perhaps, becoming less popular. Still, one can have great respect for the present Catholic Church and still criticize the Catholic Church of the Middle Ages.

Of course the Roman Catholic Church is headquartered in Rome.

The woman is dressed in purple and red. (17:4) The leaders of the Catholic Church are bishops and cardinals. Bishops wear purple and cardinals wear red.

The Catholic Church was founded by Christ, but in the Middle Ages it became corrupt. The Inquisition was created to stamp out any who tried to reform the church, killing thousands of Protestants and other reformers. The Catholic Church killed more people for being genuine Christians than either the Jews or the Romans. They turned the church into a vehicle to bring wealth and political power to the people who controlled it. So depicting the Catholic Church as a prostitute makes some sense: instead of serving Jehovah God, she was selling out for money.

Some commentators connect the Prostitute of Babylon with the woman with a crown of stars in chapter 12. They see the woman in chapter 12 as the "primitive church", the church as Christ created it. Then by chapter 17 she has become the corrupt church of the Middle Ages.

Not surprisingly, this theory is not so popular among Catholics!

A theory more common among Catholics, though not exclusively limited to Catholics, is that the Prostitute is corrupt Judaism.

Revelation 17:18 says that this woman represents a "great city", and Revelation 11:8 says that the city where "our Lord was crucified", which must mean Jerusalem, is a "great city". So as both are "great cities", they must be the same place. But surely there can be more than one great city in the world.

Similarly, the woman is called a prostitute. Isaiah 1:21 calls Jerusalem a prostitute. But again, just because two women are both called prostitutes doesn't mean they are the same person.

Advocates of this theory say that according to Revelation, the Beast destroys this city, the Beast represents the Roman Empire, and historically Rome destroyed Jerusalem.

But this is weak on many levels. For starters, Revelation does *not* say that the Beast destroys the Prostitute's city. Indeed if you study Revelation 16-18, it doesn't say exactly who destroys this city or how. We are told that an angel announces that Babylon is destroyed and that this is God's judgement, but the text doesn't say whether this is a direct judgment from God, like Sodom and Gomorrah, or if God uses a human agency to do it, like he used the Assyrians and (literal) Babylonians to destroy Israel. We are told that the city is destroyed in "one hour". It's not clear if this means that it literally takes only sixty minutes to totally destroy the city, or if this simply means that it happens very quickly. Some Futurists take this literally and say that it means that the city is destroyed with a nuclear attack, or some other highly destructive modern weapons. In any case, it is only a theory that the Beast is the Roman Empire. There are many competing theories.

I was unable to find any interpretation of the seven kings that fits within the "corrupt Jerusalem" theory. The plain reading would mean that seven kings would rule over Jerusalem before the end. But Jerusalem had many more than seven kings in its history. The Bible lists 23 Jewish kings who ruled in Jerusalem. We could debate whether we should count foreign kings whose power extended over Israel, like the Babylonians, Greeks, and Romans; the Herods, who were not Jewish and who were put in power by Rome, etc. But even just the 23 is already too many. Perhaps the seven kings aren't intended to start all the way back with King Saul.

Perhaps "seven kings" means not seven individual men, but seven empires. I have never read any commentator discuss this possibility, but just to spin my own mini-theory here, that does seem to fit history: there *were* seven empires that ruled Jerusalem:

1. Jebusites
2. Israel
3. Babylonians
4. Greeks (Alexander)
5. Romans
6. Muslims
7. British

And now Israel again controls it.

The most common Futurist view is that the Prostitute of Babylon is not any past or present institution, but is the false religion that will be created by the Antichrist in the future.

By this theory, the Prostitute may resemble past false religions, but this is just because there are features that may be found in many false religions. The Prostitute is compared to Babylon because Babylon was a place where false religion was powerful.

6.25. False Prophet

Revelation 13:11-15. Then I saw another beast coming up out of the earth, and he had two horns like a lamb and spoke like a dragon. And he exercises all the authority of the first beast in his presence, and causes the earth and those who dwell in it to worship the first beast, whose deadly wound was healed. He performs great signs, so that he even makes fire come down from heaven on the earth in the sight of men. And he deceives those who dwell on the earth by those signs which he was granted to do in the sight of the beast, telling those who dwell on the earth to make an image to the beast who was wounded by the sword and lived. He was granted *power* to give breath to the image of the beast, that the image of the beast should both speak and cause as many as would not worship the image of the beast to be killed.

Revelation 16:13-14. And I saw three unclean spirits like frogs *coming* out of the mouth of the dragon, out of the mouth of the beast, and out of the mouth of the false prophet. For they are spirits of demons, performing signs, *which* go out to the kings of the earth and of the whole world, to gather them to the battle of that great day of God Almighty.

Revelation 19:20. Then the beast was captured, and with him the false prophet who worked signs in his presence, by which he deceived those who received the mark of the beast and those who worshiped his image. These two were cast alive into the lake of fire burning with brimstone.

Revelation 20:10. The devil, who deceived them, was cast into the lake of fire and brimstone where the beast and the false prophet *are*. And they will be tormented day and night forever and ever.

Almost all commentators connect the "beast from the Earth" of Revelation 13 to the "false prophet" of Revelation 16, 19, and 20. Revelation 13 describes three beings: the dragon, the beast from the earth, and the beast from the sea. Then Revelation 16 and following refer to the dragon, the beast, and the false prophet. It seems likely that if two members of the group are the same, that the third is also, and we've just shifted to a different title. Revelation 13 says the beast from the earth performs signs and forces people to wear a mark. Revelation 19 says the false prophet performs signs and forces people to wear a mark. The similarity in the descriptions fits the idea that it's the same person.

One could reply that if they are the same person, why did the title change?

Some link the false prophet to:

Matthew 24:9-11. Then they will deliver you up to tribulation and kill you, and you will be hated by all nations for My name's sake. And then many will be offended, will betray one another, and will hate one another. Then many false prophets will rise up and deceive many.

Matthew 24:23-24. Then if anyone says to you, 'Look, here *is* the Christ!' or 'There!' do not believe *it*. For false christs and false prophets will rise and show great signs and wonders to deceive, if possible, even the elect.

1 John 4:1-3. Beloved, do not believe every spirit, but test the spirits, whether they are of God; because many false prophets have gone out into the world. By this you know the Spirit of God: Every spirit that confesses that Jesus Christ has come in the flesh is of God, and every spirit that does not confess that Jesus Christ has come in the flesh is not of God. And this is the *spirit* of the Antichrist, which you have heard was coming, and is now already in the world.

The descriptions are surely consistent: all use the words "false prophet" and talk about deceiving people, and Matthew 24:24 talks about this false prophet performing miraculous signs just like the false prophet of Revelation.

On the other hand, these descriptions are pretty general. There have been many people over the millennia who could accurately be called "false prophets".

The fact that Matthew 24 and Revelation both talk about a false prophet is evidence that they are discussing the same events. Jesus, as quoted here, doesn't really tell us a lot about this false prophet. So if he is talking about the same person, the main value of it may be to link Matthew 24 to Revelation.

1 John 4 clearly says "many false prophets": he is not talking about one particular false prophet. John may intend for his discussion of "many false prophets" to specifically include *the* false prophet of Revelation. But really his comments appear to be about false prophets in general, about all false prophets from the time of Christ on. Taken that way, he gives us some general information applicable to all false prophets. Perhaps the

most important point being that you can recognize false prophets because they deny Christ.

Some commentators see a parallel between this "team" of the dragon, the Beast, and the false prophet and the Trinity. That is, perhaps this is Satan's "Unholy Trinity". The dragon tries to take the place of God the Father; the Beast of God the Son, Jesus; and the false prophet of the Holy Spirit. The parallel seems too close to be coincidence. It might be that Satan is mocking God. It might be that the same reasons that make the Holy Trinity a useful thing also make the Unholy Trinity a useful thing.

Note that the Beast comes from "the sea", while the false prophet comes from "the earth". This appears to be significant, but it is not spelled out just what the significance is.

Revelation 12:13-18 also mentions earth and sea. Again, they are probably symbols for something, but it is not clear what.

Some point to Revelation 17:15, which, speaking of the Prostitute of Babylon (see section 6.24), says, "The waters which you saw, where the harlot sits, are peoples, multitudes, nations, and tongues." So perhaps the waters that the Beast comes from represent many nations. But then what does the earth that the false prophet comes from represent?

Another theory is that the sea represents Europe, because Jews had to travel by sea to get there; while the earth represents the Middle East, because Jews could reach it by land. By that theory, the Beast is from Europe, and the False Prophet is from the Middle East. Perhaps the Beast is a European ruler, and the False Prophet is Muhammad or a later Muslim ruler. Plausible, I suppose, but there's no scriptural evidence for it.

There's little debate that the term "false prophet" is literal: he is a religious leader who tells lies. He is able to perform miracles. Most commentators say that he performs miracles through the power of Satan. Another possibility is that he is simply a fraud who is able to convince people that he can perform miracles but they're simply parlor tricks, like modern psychics. Either way, he convinces people to worship the Beast as if the beast was God.

6.26. Two Witnesses

Revelation 11:3-12. "And I will give *power* to my two witnesses, and they will prophesy one thousand two hundred and sixty days, clothed in sackcloth." These are the two olive trees and the two lampstands standing before the God of the earth. And if anyone wants to harm them, fire proceeds from their mouth and devours their enemies. And if anyone wants to harm them, he must be killed in this manner. These have power to shut heaven, so that no rain falls in the days of their prophecy; and they have power over waters to turn them to blood, and to strike the earth with all plagues, as often as they desire. When they finish their testimony, the beast that ascends out of the bottomless pit will make war against them, overcome them, and kill them. And their dead bodies *will lie* in the street of the great city which spiritually is called Sodom and Egypt, where also our Lord was crucified. Then *those* from the peoples, tribes, tongues, and nations will see their dead bodies three-and-a-half days, and not allow their dead bodies to be put into graves. And those who dwell on the earth will rejoice over them, make merry, and send gifts to one another, because these two prophets tormented those who dwell on the earth. Now after the three-and-a-half days the breath of life from God entered them, and they stood on their feet, and great fear fell on those who saw them. And they heard a loud voice from heaven saying to them, "Come up here." And they ascended to heaven in a cloud, and their enemies saw them.

The obvious question is, Who are these "two witnesses"?

Theory 1: Moses and Elijah. The miracles they perform resemble those done by Moses and Elijah.

Revelation 11:6a says that they can stop the rain. 1 King 17:1 says that Elijah stopped the rain. 11:6b says that they turn water to blood. Exodus 7:19 says that Moses turned water to blood.

Moses and Elijah appeared at the time of Jesus's first coming.

Matthew 17:1,3. Now after six days Jesus took Peter, James, and John his brother, led them up on a high mountain by themselves; ... And behold, Moses and Elijah appeared to them, talking with Him.

If they came back to Earth for his first coming, maybe they will return again at his Second Coming.

Personally I find this weak. Yes, the Witnesses perform a miracle that is similar to one done through Elijah and another that is similar to one done through Moses. But it was not Elijah and Moses who performed the miracle, but God. Surely God is capable of performing the same miracle using a different person. It's not like God is there in Heaven saying, "I need to turn water to blood. Hmm, who do I know who can do that?" Furthermore, they perform other miracles that do not resemble anything done by Moses or Elijah.

Some point out that God said that Elijah would return:

Malachi 4:5. Behold, I will send you Elijah the prophet before the coming of the great and dreadful day of the LORD.

But Jesus said that this prophecy was fulfilled in John the Baptist:

Matthew 11:13-14. For all the prophets and the law prophesied until John. And if you are willing to receive *it*, he is Elijah who is to come.

So when the prophet Malachi said that Elijah would return, this did not mean that he would be reincarnated or that his spirit would come down from Heaven or anything blatantly miraculous. Rather, it meant that a man who was *like* Elijah would come to prepare the way for Christ.

So even if we make much of the similarity between the miracles of Moses and Elijah and the miracles of the Two Witnesses, this may just be that God is sending two men who are *like* these great prophets of Old Testament times.

Theory 2: Enoch and Elijah. These are the only two

people recorded in the Old Testament who never died.

> Hebrews 11:5. By faith Enoch was taken away so that he did not see death, "and was not found, because God had taken him".

> 2 Kings 2:11. Then it happened, as they continued on and talked, that suddenly a chariot of fire *appeared* with horses of fire, and separated the two of them; and Elijah went up by a whirlwind into heaven.

If these two men were taken up to Heaven without ever dying, perhaps that was because God intended for them to return and continue their work.

Theory 3: Two other guys. Nowhere does the Bible say that Moses, Elijah, or Enoch are returning at the time of the Second Coming. Perhaps the Witnesses are simply two men living at the time of the Second Coming, whom God chooses to use. God has used people throughout history, without having to send the same people back over and over. We don't generally suppose that Martin Luther or Billy Graham must have been Old Testament prophets brought back to life.

Theory 4: Two churches. 11:4 says that the Two Witnesses are two lampstands. Revelation 1:20 says that lampstands represent churches. If just a few pages before we are told that lampstands represent churches, then it seems reasonable to conclude that they represent the same thing here.

By this theory, they are not two individual men but two congregations, and the persecution of them is not persecution of just two men but widespread persecution of Christians.

The main problem with this theory is that the rest of the text in Revelation 11 sounds like it is talking about two individuals, not two churches. Especially when it says that God brings them back to life after they are killed. This could mean that two churches are destroyed and God then revives them. But the plain reading of the text, when it talks about people being amazed and afraid when the two witnesses are brought back to life, makes more sense if it's talking about two individuals. If a human being was killed and God brought him back to life, people would likely be amazed and afraid. But if a church was destroyed and then revived, not really so amazing.

Perhaps when Revelation talks about the witnesses being killed, it means a number of people. Many Christians are killed, their dead bodies are left lying in the streets for 3 ½ days, etc. That would mean that the prophecy is shifting from talking about two churches to the people who make up those churches, but that isn't necessarily extraordinary or even awkward.

If they are two churches, there are two sub-theories.

Theory 4A: Two of the Seven Churches from Revelation 2 and 3. As the Two Witnesses are killed at the same time, this is not compatible with a theory that the Seven Churches are an historical progression. Unless, perhaps, we suppose that at the time of the seventh church, elements of the sixth church still exist. This may be referring to two separate times of persecution, but that seems to really be stretching the text.

Theory 4B: These are simply two churches that exist at the time of the Second Coming. If the Seven Churches are church types that will exist throughout history, then this would be about the same as saying that they are two of the seven.

Theory 5: Similar to Theory 4, the two witnesses are Christians and Jews.

Oh, in case you're wondering: At the beginning of this book I said that there was only one question where I was previously undecided but where after doing the research for this book I came to a conclusion. This is it. I now think Theory 4 is correct.

6.27. Man on the White Horse

There are two men in Revelation described as conquerors on white horses:

Revelation 6:1-2. Now I saw when the Lamb opened one of the seals; and I heard one of the four living creatures saying with a voice like thunder, "Come and see." And I looked, and behold, a white horse. He who sat on it had a bow; and a crown was given to him, and he went out conquering and to conquer.

Revelation 19:11-13, 16. Now I saw heaven opened, and behold, a white horse. And He who sat on him *was* called Faithful and True, and in righteousness He judges and makes war. His eyes *were* like a flame of fire, and on His head *were* many crowns. He had a name written that no one knew except Himself. He *was* clothed with a robe dipped in blood, and His name is called The Word of God. ... And He has on *His* robe and on His thigh a name written: KING OF KINGS AND LORD OF LORDS.

All commentators that I have consulted agree that the man in Revelation 19 is Christ. He is "the Word of God", a title given to Jesus in John 1. He is "Faithful and True", and the armies of Heaven follow him. Etc. It is hard to imagine how this description would fit anyone other than Jesus.

But there is debate about the identity of the man in Revelation 6.

Theory 1: The less popular theory is that the horseman of Revelation 6 is also Christ. There are a number of similarities between the two descriptions. Most obviously, both are men on white horses. Both wear a crown. Both go to war and are victorious.

Theory 2: But most modern commentators say that these are two different people: The man in 19 is Christ, but the man in 6 is the Antichrist.

They point to differences in the description: The man in 19 has a sword, but the man in 6 has a bow. The man in 19 has many crowns, but the man in 6 has only 1 crown. Also, the words used to describe the crown are different: Chapter 6 uses the Greek word ΣΤΕΦΑΝΟΣ ("stephanos"), which means a laurel wreath. In ancient times a crown made of laurel leaves and woven into a sort of wreath to fit on someone's head was often awarded to a conquering general or to the winner of an athletic competition. Of course the former is relevant here: he is given a laurel wreath to show that he has won the war. By the way, this is where we get the phrase "don't rest on your laurels". If you won a laurel wreath in some competition, presumably because you worked hard and trained and practiced, you shouldn't now use that laurel wreath as a cushion to rest on. You should keep working and accomplish more. Chapter 19 uses ΔΙΑΔΗΜΑΤΑ ("diademata"), which means "diadems", or metal crowns with embedded jewels. This was a kind of crown that would be worn by a king.

Some also say that the horseman in chapter 6 cannot be Christ because his description comes in a section where Christ is reading these things from a scroll.

> Revelation 5:2-4. Then I saw a strong angel proclaiming with a loud voice, "Who is worthy to open the scroll and to loose its seals?" And no one in heaven or on the earth or under the earth was able to open the scroll, or to look at it. So I wept much, because no one was found worthy to open and read the scroll, or to look at it. But one of the elders said to me, "Do not weep. Behold, the Lion of the tribe of Judah, the Root of David, has prevailed to open the scroll and to loose its seven seals."

How can Christ be reading the scroll, and at the same time be a participant in the events it describes?

Furthermore, Revelation 6:1 says that the horseman is summoned by one of "the four living creatures" – "the four beasts" in many older translations – which appear to be some sort of angels or angel-like creatures. But how could any created being summon Christ? Creatures can't give orders to their Creator.

These two points don't seem very strong. Why couldn't a person read a book in which he himself is mentioned? I'm sure the president reads news stories about himself every day. It's not at all hard to imagine some famous person saying to a friend or co-worker, "Listen to what this newspaper is saying about me!", and then proceeding to read the story.

Some interpret this not just that Jesus is reading the book, but that the events happen as he reads. This gets us tangled in the mechanics of the prophecy. Was Jesus telling John what would happen in the future, and then showing him scenes like video clips? Or did he actually transport John to the future to see it happen?

On the last point, we could debate if a created being could not "summon" Christ in some sense. People routinely pray, "Jesus, please be with us today ..." But in any case it's not relevant. Read the text carefully. It doesn't say that the living creature summons the horseman. It says that the living creature summons John to come and see the horseman.

6.28. Number of the Beast

Perhaps the best known passage in Revelation is the discussion of the "number of the beast".

> Revelation 13:17-18. and that no one may buy or sell except one who has the mark or the name of the beast, or the number of his name. Here is wisdom. Let him who has understanding calculate the number of the beast, for it is the number of a man: His number *is* 666.

Some people come up with elaborate theories about where this number comes from. But to any ancient-Greek-speaking person, that is obvious. In ancient Greek, they use the same symbols for numbers that they use for letters. Basically, the first 9 letters are the numbers 1 to 9, the next nine letters are 10 to 90, and the next 9 are 100 to 900. The Greek alphabet only has 24 letters so they used 3 obsolete letters to fill it out to 27. See Figure 3. (The ones where I put the English equivalent in parentheses are those where the Greeks used obsolete letters.)

They put a mark in front of a letter, called a "left keraia", to mean "times 1000". This was a small tick mark placed low on the line, resembling a modern comma. So for example β, the second letter of the alphabet, is normally 2, but with the extra mark it is 2000. This got them up to 999,999. They had no

Figure 3		
Greek Letter	English Equivalent	Value
α	a	1
β	b	2
γ	g	3
δ	d	4
ε	e	5
ς	(f)	6
ζ	z	7
η	e	8
θ	th	9
ι	i	10
κ	k	20
λ	l	30
μ	m	40
ν	n	50
ξ	x	60
ο	o	70
π	p	80
५	(k)	90
ρ	r	100
σ	s	200
τ	t	300
υ	u/y	400
φ	ph	500
χ	ch	600
ψ	ps	700
ω	oo	800
⟩	(s)	900

systematic way for representing larger numbers, but would talk about "a thousand thousands" and the like.

Typically they would write the "digits" for the largest value first. So for example, 823 would be ωκγ. But unlike our Hindu-Arabic numerals, position does not determine value, so ωκγ is the same as γωκ or κγω or any other order.

So the Greeks couldn't help but see numbers in everything they wrote. Every word looked like a number.

It would be like in English if we said A=1, B=2, C=3, ... I=9, J=10, K=20, L=30, ... R=90, S=100, T=200, ... Z=800, and then added another symbol for 900. If you wrote the word DOG, you would just naturally see it as 4+60+7=71. You would automatically think of 71 as being the number of a dog. You would think of the number 495 as a very romantic number, because it can be written LOVE. And so on, for any word you wrote.

So when John said that the "number of his name" is 666, any Greek reading his book would instantly understand that to mean that if you add up the number values of the letters in his name, it comes to 666.

Some try to look for mystical significance in this number.

For example, some say that 6 is the number of man, because man was created on the 6th day, and 3 is the number of God, because God is a trinity. Thus 666 is man making himself God. Possible, but nowhere does the Bible say any of this. It's just speculation. Even if true, it doesn't tell us anything we didn't already know. And if someone did offer an explanation of the significance of 666 that gave us new information, it would be unreliable because it would just be speculation with no scripture to back it up.

Many people have added up the values of some famous person's name and claimed that it came to 666. We should be cautious about jumping to the conclusion that someone is the Antichrist just because his name adds up to this total. There are 7 billion people in the world today, many more billions who have lived. But most people's names will only add up to 1000 or so. That is, there are only about 1000 different totals. So there are likely millions of people in the world whose names will add up to 666 just by chance. Not all of them are the Antichrist!

The Jews also used their letters for numbers, in a system very similar to the Greeks. Using the Hebrew spelling of "Nero Ceasar", נרון קסר and the Hebrew number system, Nero's name adds up to 666. See Figure 4.

Figure 4			
Hebrew Letter	**Name**	**English Equivalent**	**Value**
נ	nun	n	50
ר	resh	r	200
ו	vav	v/o	6
נ	nun	n	50
ק	qaf	k/c	100
ס	samekh	s	60
ר	resh	r	200
		total	666

I've seen lots of calculations showing that one person's

name or another's adds up to 666. Among the people who add up to 666, if you do the calculation right, are:

Caligula, the Roman emperor
Trajan, another Roman emperor
Muhammad
Various popes (according to Protestants)
Martin Luther (according to Catholics)
Napoleon
Adolf Hitler
Henry Kissinger
Barack Obama
Donald Trump
Etc

And when I say "do the calculation right", that's the trick. Should we translate the person's name into Greek? How about Hebrew? Or we could make up a system to assign numbers to letters in English (like I did above to illustrate how Greek works). Do we take just the last name, first and last, or include the middle name? Do we include a title like "Mr" or "General"? I've seen many calculations that deliberately mis-spell the person's name to make it work. Or that add all sorts of manipulations – "now multiply by 3 and add 7" and the like – with little justification beyond it being necessary to come to the right total.

For example, here's one calculation I saw to make Barack Obama add up to 666:

A=1, B=2, C=3, D=4, E=5, F=6, G=7, H=8, I=9, J=10, K=11, L=12, M= 13, N=14, O=15, P=16, Q=17, R=18, S=19, T=20, U=21, V=22, W=23, X=24, Y=25, Z=26.

Barack: 2+1+18+1+3+11=36
Hussein: 8+21+19+19+5+9+14=95
Obama: 15+2+1+13+1=32
Add these: 36+95+32=163.
Multiply by the Beast: 163 x 666 = 108,558.

Split and Add: 108 + 558 = 666.

Amusing, but where did that "multiply by the Beast" and "split and add" come from? Did whoever come up with this start out saying that, after careful Bible study, this was the formula that should be applied, and then he was startled to discover that Obama added up to 666? Or is it more likely that he decided first that Obama must add up to 666, and then tinkered with the numbers until he came up with some formula that worked? Maybe whoever came up with this formula didn't think to try this, but plug other numbers into this "multiply by 666, split at the thousands separator, and add". Try 1, 2, 3, etc. Notice something interesting? Run *any* number from 1 to 999 through this formula and they all add up to either 333, 666, 999, or 1332. (I wrote a quick little computer program to try it. Extra credit if you can construct a mathematical proof that this is true.) So about one out of every four people in the world will come out to 666 using this formula.

If you tinker with how you assign numbers to letters and how you manipulate them, I'm sure you can come up with some rules under which almost anyone will add up to 666.

Similarly, I have heard many claims to have proven that someone is the Beast because the speaker found the number 666 connected to the person in some way. Just recently someone showed me a document claiming that Donald Trump is the Beast, because his address is 666 Fifth Avenue in Manhattan. Furthermore, the document said, he paid $1.8 billion for this building, and 1.8 = 3 x 6 = 666.

There is so much wrong with this that I hardly know where to begin.

Donald Trump does not own the building at 666 Fifth Avenue. His son-in-law, Jared Kushner, owns the building. Nowhere does Revelation say that the number of the Beast's son-in-law is 666. Neither Trump nor Kushner live there.

1,800,000,000 is *not* equal to 3 x 6. It is equal to 3 x 600,000,000. And nowhere does the Bible associate the beast with the number 600000000600000000600000000. I don't know the details of the real estate deal, but I doubt the price was *exactly* $1,800,000,000.00. If this is just a round number and the actual number is a little more or less, than the calculation falls apart.

But most important, the Bible says that 666 is "the number of his name". It is not his address or the amount he paid for something or his height or his SAT score. You can't comb through every number that you can possibly connect to someone looking for one that is 666, or that you can manipulate according to some formula so that it comes to 666.

Think of all the numbers that someone could associate with you: your height, weight, address, phone number, bank account numbers, credit cards, birth date, distance you drive to work every day, etc, etc. Bear in mind that any length or height could be expressed in feet, inches, meters, cubits, etc., creating many more numbers. If someone looked long and hard enough, they could surely find one of these numbers that happens to be 666, or that has three sixes in it, or that they can run through some formula that they just made up so that the result comes out to 666.

So when someone tells me that some contemporary figure is the Beast because he found the number 666 somewhere around him ... I am not impressed. I rather doubt that either Barack Obama or Donald Trump is the Beast. I am certainly not convinced by these calculations.

Let me end with a few related numbers:

999: the number of the Beast in Australian Bibles
668: the next door neighbor of the Beast
665.95: the number of the Beast in retail stores

7. Final Thoughts

7.1. Purpose of Prophecy

What is the purpose of prophecy? Why did God include prophecies in the Bible?

I've quoted Isaac Newton a few times in this book. He's a hero to me: probably the greatest scientist who ever lived, and also a devout, Bible-believing Christian. He offered this theory on why God gave us prophecies:

> The folly of Interpreters has been, to foretel times and things by this Prophecy, as if God designed to make them Prophets. By this rashness they have not only exposed themselves, but brought the Prophecy also into contempt. The design of God was much otherwise. He gave this and the Prophecies of the Old Testament, not to gratify men's curiosities by enabling them to foreknow things, but that after they were fulfilled they might be interpreted by the event, and his own Providence, not the Interpreters, be then manifested thereby to the world. For the event of things predicted many ages before, will then be a convincing argument that the world is

governed by providence. For as the few and obscure Prophecies concerning Christ's first coming were for setting up the Christian religion, which all nations have since corrupted; so the many and clear Prophecies concerning the things to be done at Christ's second coming, are not only for predicting but also for effecting a recovery and re-establishment of the long-lost truth, and setting up a kingdom wherein dwells righteousness. The event will prove the Apocalypse; and this Prophecy, thus proved and understood, will open the old Prophets, and all together will make known the true religion, and establish it. For he that will understand the old Prophets, must begin with this; but the time is not yet come for understanding them perfectly, because the main revolution predicted in them is not yet come to pass. In the days of the voice of the seventh Angel, when he shall begin to sound, the mystery of God shall be finished, as he hath declared to his servants the Prophets: and then the kingdoms of this world shall become the kingdoms of our Lord and his Christ, and he shall reign for ever, Apoc. x. 7. xi. 15. There is already so much of the Prophecy fulfilled, that as many as will take pains in this study, may see sufficient instances of God's providence: but then the signal revolutions predicted by all the holy Prophets, will at once both turn mens eyes upon considering the predictions, and plainly interpret them. Till then we must content ourselves with interpreting what hath been already fulfilled.

— Isaac Newton, *Observations Upon the Prophecies of Daniel, and the Apocalypse of St. John*, Part 2
Chapter 1

Newton believed that the purpose of prophecy is not that we may know the future, but that after it happens, when we see the fulfillment, we will see that God knew the future, and our faith will be strengthened.

I've had many conversations with atheists where they say,

If God is real, why doesn't he perform this miracle or that miracle, and then everyone would have to believe.

For example, every now and then an atheist will say, If God really exists, why doesn't he strike me with lightning right now for my blasphemy?

Suppose that at that very moment a bolt of lightning tore through the roof, hit the speaker, and knocked him to the ground. Would this lead all the atheists in the world to suddenly believe in God?

I doubt it. Assuming the person wasn't seriously hurt, I'm sure they would all quickly be laughing, "Wow, what a bizarre coincidence! Just as he said that …" If Christians spread the story, atheists would be denying it ever happened. Even if someone had a video and posted it on YouTube, atheists would be writing articles proving that the video was a fake. If you doubt that, just look at the response to various Christian claims of contemporary miracles.

Fulfilled prophecy is hard to refute. It's right there, on the record, and you need only look at the history books to see that it was fulfilled. Not that atheists don't ignore it, of course. And they have all sorts of tortured rebuttals. When I was in college, one of my professors said that Daniel could not have been written until centuries after the date normally given to this book. His proof: The prophecies in Daniel are too specific and accurate, and as of course it is impossible to predict the future, the book could not have been written until after the events described. Case closed. He struggled with how to date Daniel after the Roman Empire – that was too big a stretch even for his history-mangling – so he solved that problem by saying that the section of Daniel's prophecy that describes the Roman Empire was not about the Roman Empire, but about some other empire that never existed. So Daniel gets no points for accurately describing Rome, and then he loses more points for describing some fictional empire that never existed.

But they have to work hard to explain it away. If someone says that God cured his cancer, the atheist can always reply that you are lying and you never had cancer. If you produce medical records to prove it, he can say that you probably just recovered through routine medical treatment.

But fulfilled prophecy is hard to explain away. It's right there in print, and it has been there for hundreds or thousands of years, and the fulfillment is in hundreds of secular history books.

Another reason is to give us hope for the future. The Bible assures us that God will win in the end. No matter how bad things seem right now, God is in control.

It must be very depressing, even frightening, to be an honest atheist. He has to believe that he is at the mercy of all sorts of forces beyond his control. There are random forces like natural disasters and disease. There are human institutions that care nothing about him, like the government or huge corporations or the global economy. Some of these forces may even be actively hostile to him, like political parties he opposes. There is little he can do about any of these. He is a helpless victim of the universe. And in the end, one way or another, he will die and thus, he believes, cease to exist. For 99.99+% of human beings, within a generation or two no one will even remember that he ever lived. That must be absolutely terrifying. Many atheists engage in psychological tricks to avoid this, like saying, "Well, I think in the end everything works out for the best." But why should it? You've carefully explained to us that the universe is controlled by random forces and fallible humans. What would cause things to work out for the best? Or, "People get what they deserve." But the whole point of atheism is that there is no force in the universe that ensures that people get what they deserve.

But as a Christian, any time I have problems in life, I have confidence that God is in control. If I lose my job or my wife threatens to leave me, God can solve this problem. If in his sovereignty he does not resolve it the way I wanted, still, I am assured that one day I will be resurrected and live for eternity in Paradise with him. Long term, there's nothing to worry about.

Fulfilled prophecies about the past give me confidence

that God's word is accurate. Prophecies about the future assure me that God is in control and that the good guys win in the end.

7.2. Knowing the Truth

Sometimes Christians say that there are things that we are just not meant to know and so we shouldn't waste time thinking about them. Every now and then someone says that it is arrogant and presumptuous to try to learn things that "man was not meant to know". I've read books that were written back in the 1940s and 1950s, where people were so frightened by the destructive power of the atom bomb that they worried that it was a sin to try to learn things that God didn't want us to know.

I disagree. There was a line in the old movie, *Battle for the Planet of the Apes* (1973), where a character says, "All knowledge is for good. Only the use to which you put it can be good or evil." (http://www.imdb.com/title/tt0069768/quotes) -- I thought a very true and profound statement from an otherwise very forgettable movie.

What do we gain by studying prophecy? If nothing else, it is always good to know more about God and his will, and to study his word.

We need to be careful not to get arrogant about our theories. I heard about a Christian organization that had written a book explaining end times prophecies and relating them to current events. They were trying to print many copies and distribute them around so that after the Rapture, people would find their book and would see how all this was predicted in the Bible. I thought that rather presumptuous and foolish. I never read their book, but frankly, I think the probability that they interpreted prophecy so accurately that people will be shocked by its dead-on precision is pretty small. If I've convinced you of nothing else with this book, I hope you are convinced that people who have theories about prophecy that conflict with what you have been taught are often honest Christians who can give solid, Biblical arguments for their position that are at least coherent.

It is said that there are over 300 prophecies in the Old Testament that were fulfilled by Jesus. (I've never counted them, but I'll take other's word on the number.) And yet when Jesus came, very few had correctly predicted when and where he would arrive. The only people who showed up for his birth were shepherds who had been given a special revelation, and magi from the East. Jewish priests and scribes who had studied the Bible their entire lives were noticeably absent.

Likewise, when Jesus comes again, I suspect that most Christians will be surprised. We will suddenly discover that the prophecy that we thought was intended literally was really symbolic or vice versa, that the description that we thought fit 21st century Europe perfectly was really talking about 22nd century Korea, or whatever.

I can think of many things that Christians have said about the Bible through the centuries that I think are clearly wrong. I sometimes wonder, are there things that I believe because that's what I was taught in Sunday School or I read it in a book somewhere or heard from a preacher on the radio, that are in fact not in the Bible at all or that are gross misinterpretations of things in the Bible, but I've never thought to question them but take them as obvious truth?

Let me make clear that I'm not saying that we should despair of ever knowing the truth. Rather, I am saying that we should study hard and be willing to question assumptions, and not get arrogant and assume we already know it all.

May God be with you in your own studies. I hope and pray that this book has been helpful to you in some small way.

Keep the faith.

Index

www.ingramcontent.com/pod-product-compliance
Lightning Source LLC
LaVergne TN
LVHW041153080426
835511LV00006B/575